BRIG

BLEAK HOUSE BY CHARLES DICKENS

Intelligent Education

INFLUENCE PUBLISHERS

Nashville, Tennessee

BRIGHT NOTES: Bleak House

www.BrightNotes.com

No part of this publication may be used or reproduced in any manner whatsoever without written permission, except in the case of brief quotations in critical articles and reviews. For permissions, contact Influence Publishers http://www.influencepublishers.com.

ISBN: 978-1-645420-50-7 (Paperback)
ISBN: 978-1-645420-51-4 (eBook)

Published in accordance with the U.S. Copyright Office Orphan Works and Mass Digitization report of the register of copyrights, June 2015.

Originally published by Monarch Press.
Edward R. Winans, 1964
2019 Edition published by Influence Publishers.

Interior design by Lapiz Digital Services. Cover Design by Thinkpen Designs.

Printed in the United States of America.

Library of Congress Cataloging-in-Publication Data forthcoming.
Names: Intelligent Education
Title: BRIGHT NOTES: Bleak House
Subject: STU004000 STUDY AIDS / Book Notes

CONTENTS

INTRODUCTION TO CHARLES DICKENS

. . . .

EARLY LIFE

Charles Dickens was born on February 7, 1812, in Portsea. His father, John Dickens, was a minor clerk in the Navy Pay Office; his father's parents had been servants and his mother's parents only slightly higher on the social scale. John Dickens was a happy-go-lucky, improvident man whose family often knew want as the debts piled up. At the age of twelve, Charles Dickens experienced what was to become the key event of his life. His father was imprisoned for debt in the Marshalsea Prison; young Charles was taken out of school and put to work in a blacking warehouse in London, pasting labels on bottles of shoe polish. Although he later returned to school for a time, this experience left a permanent mark on the soul of Charles Dickens. Even many years later, after he had become a successful author, he could not bear to talk about it, or be reminded of his family's ignominy.

At the age of fifteen Dickens began working as an office boy for a law firm. He taught himself shorthand and by 1828 he became a reporter for the lay courts of Doctors' Common. The dull routine of the legal profession never interested him, so he became a newspaper reporter for the *Mirror of Parliament*, *The True Sun*, and finally for the *Morning Chronicle*. (John Forster, later his closest friend and biographer, was also employed at

The True Sun.) By the age of twenty, Dickens was one of the best Parliamentary reporters in all England.

During this same period Dickens' interest began to switch from journalism to literature. His first work of fiction, "Dinner at Poplar Walk" (later reprinted as "Mr. Minns and His Cousin"), appeared in the *Monthly Magazine* when he was twenty-one. His newspaper work had given him an intimate knowledge of the streets and byways of London, and late in 1832 he began writing sketches and stories of London life. They began to appear in periodicals and newspapers in 1833, and in 1836 were gathered together as *Sketches by Boz, Illustrations of Every-day Life*, and *Every-day People*. This pseudonym, Boz, was suggested by his brother's pronunciation of "Moses" when he had a cold.

PICKWICK PAPERS

The success of the Sketches brought an invitation from the publishers Chapman and Hall in 1836 to furnish the "letter-press" for a series of cartoon sketches about a humorous cockney sporting club. (The letter-press was little more than a running accompaniment, like an ornamental border around the drawings.) The project had hardly begun when Robert Seymour, the artist, committed suicide. Dickens searched long for a new artist and found an ideal collaborator in H. K. Browne ("Phiz"), but Dickens had persuaded the publisher to let him improvise a fictional narrative. When the *Posthumous Papers* of the *Pickwick Club* finally came out, the story predominated over the illustrations.

When *Pickwick Papers* appeared in April, 1836, as a monthly serial, the sales were at first discouraging. Of the first issue, a modest 400 copies were printed; later the work became increasingly popular. Some 40,000 copies of each issue were sold. After the last installment appeared in November, 1837, the novel was published in book form. This set the pattern for all of Dickens' subsequent novels.

The success of *Pickwick* convinced Dickens that his real career lay in writing fiction; he gave up his Parliamentary reporting in order to devote himself full time to it. In 1836 he had married Catherine Hogarth, the daughter of one of the owners of the *Morning Chronicle*; his growing family made it necessary to work exhaustingly at his writing. His next work, *Oliver Twist*, began appearing even before *Pickwick* was completed. *Nicholas Nickleby* followed in a like manner in 1838–39, and the very first number sold some 50,000 copies. During this same period he was editor of Bentley's *Miscellany* (1837–39). By the 1840s Dickens had become the most popular novelist in Britain, taking over the place long held by Sir Walter Scott.

THE MIDDLE YEARS

The years between 1840 and 1855 were most fruitful ones: *The Old Curiosity Shop, Barnaby Rudge, A Christmas Carol, Martin Chuzzlewit, Dombey and Son, David Copperfield, Bleak House, Little Dorritt*, and *Hard Times* all appeared. In addition, he made his first trip to America; copyright laws at that time allowed American publishers to pirate his works, and their lack of concern over this injustice undoubtedly contributed to Dickens' unfavorable criticism of America in *Martin Chuzzlewit*. In 1850 Dickens founded his own periodical, *Household Words*, and continued to edit it until he and his partner exchanged it for *All the Year Round* in 1859. *Hard Times, A Tale of Two Cities*, and *Great Expectations* appeared in serial form in these publications. But these years of literary success were marred by domestic strife. He and his wife had never been particularly suited to each other, and their marriage ended in separation in 1856.

In addition to writing, Dickens had another love - amateur theatricals - which led him into yet another pursuit in the latter part of his career. He gave public readings from his novels from 1859 to 1868 in England, Scotland, and America. He had always loved the theater - he studied drama as a young man and had organized an amateur theatrical company of his own in 1847 (he was both manager and principal actor).

His energies never seemed to fail: he burned the candle at both ends. He published *Our Mutual Friend* in 1864–65 and at his death left an unfinished novel, *The Mystery of Edwin Drood*, a suspense tale in the nature of a detective story. He died suddenly in 1870 from a stroke at the age of fifty-eight. G. K. Chesterton once said that Dickens died of "popularity." It would seem so; his exhaustive burden (marked by insomnia and fatigue) is well cataloged in his letters. He was buried in the Poets' Corner of Westminster Abbey.

Dickens wrote with an eye on the tastes of a wide readership, never far ahead of the printer, and was always ready to modify the story to suit his readers. For example, when the sales of serial installments of Martin Chuzzlewit fell from 60,000 to 20,000, Dickens sent his hero off to America in order to stimulate renewed interest. No novelist ever had so close a relationship with his public, a public ranging from barely literate factory girls to wealthy dowagers, but consisting mostly of the newly formed middle classes.

TEACHER AND ENTERTAINER

Walter Allen in *The English Novel* points out that Dickens became the spokesman for this rising middle class, and also its teacher. "Dickens more than any of his contemporaries was the expression of the conscience-untutored, baffled, muddled as it doubtless often was-of his age," he writes. Not only in his novels, but in his magazine, *Household Words*, Dickens lashed out at what he considered the worst social abuses of his time: imprisonment for debt, the ferocious penal code, the unsanitary slums which bred criminals, child labor, the widespread mistreatment of children, the unsafe machinery in factories, and the hideous schools.

Yet, as Allen suggests, Dickens was primarily a great entertainer, "the greatest entertainer, probably, in the history of fiction." It is significant that Dickens was not satisfied to have his books the best sellers of their time. He wanted to see his audience, to manipulate it with the power of his own words. His public readings gave him an excellent opportunity to do so. Sitting alone on a bare stage, he would read excerpts from various novels, act them out really, imitating the voices of the various characters. These theatrical readings would always contain a dying-child scene or two which left his audience limp and tear-stained. Dickens suffered all the emotions with his audience, even after repeated readings, and this undoubtedly helped to shorten his life. He entertained his readers with humor, pathos, suspense, and melodrama, all on a grand scale. Charles Dickens had a fertile imagination that peopled his novels with characters and events which continue to entertain twentieth-century readers as they delighted his contemporaries.

NOVEL TECHNIQUE

An understanding of Dickens as an artist requires an understanding of the method of publication he used-monthly or weekly installments. Serialization left its mark on his fiction and often accounts for the flaws which many critics have found in his work. John Butt and Kathleen Tillotson in *Dickens at Work* (1957) describe the problems serial publication imposed:

"Chapters must be balanced within a number in respect both of length and of effect. Each number must lead, if not to a **climax**, at least to a point of rest; and the rest between numbers is necessarily more extended than what the mere chapter divisions provide. The writer had also to bear in mind that his readers were constantly interrupted for prolonged periods, and that he must take this into account in his characterizations and, to some extent, in his plotting."

This technique brought on a loose, episodic treatment with a vast, intricate plot, numerous characters and much repetition to jog the reader's memory. Instead of the whole novel slowly building to a real **climax**, each part had to have a little **climax** of its own. In *Hard Times* the bad effects of serialization are at a minimum because it is a comparatively short novel (about 260 pages in most editions) and it appeared in weekly rather than monthly parts. But the careful reader can still tell where each part ended; considerations of space rather than of artistic technique formed the story.

The works of Dickens have many of their roots in the eighteenth century, especially in the novels of Tobias Smollett, whom he greatly admired. From Smollett he borrowed many devices of characterization - "tagging" characters with physical peculiarities, speech mannerisms, compulsive gestures, and eccentric names. Examples in *Hard Times* include the distinctive speech pattern of Stephen Blackpool, who talks in a phonetically transcribed Lancashire dialect; the self-deprecating speech of Bounderby or the self-pitying talk of Mrs. Sparsit; the physical peculiarities of Bitzer, the epitome of pallidness; the names of characters - Bounderby, M'Choakumchild, Gradgrind-so evocative of their personalities.

The eighteenth century also brought the picaresque tradition in fiction to full flower. (The term refers to novels which depict the life of a picaro [Spanish: "rogue"] and which consist of unconnected **episodes** held together by the presence of the central character.) Early novels, especially those of Defoe, Fielding, and Smollett, were rambling, episodic, and anecdotal. Many of the novels of Dickens-*Pickwick*, *Oliver Twist*, *David Copperfield* to name a few - are picaresque in technique. *Hard Times* borrows from the tradition only the irreverent, satirical view of stuffed-shirt pretentiousness and of established society in general. The eighteenth-century theater, with its sharply defined villains, its involved melodramatic plots, and its farcical humor, also suggested ideas for plots and characterizations to Dickens.

Dickens took his descriptive techniques from Sir Walter Scott and other early nineteenth-century novelists. No character, no matter how minor, appears on the scene without being fully described, not only as to physical appearance, but as to the clothing he wears. Dickens also excels in the short but evocative description of places; in *Hard Times* note the portrayal of the murky streets and factories of Coketown and of its blighted wasteland-like countryside.

THE WORLD OF HIS NOVELS

The world of Dickens' novels is a fantasy world, a fairy-tale world, a nightmare world. It is a world seen as through the eyes of a child: the shadows are blacker, the fog denser, the houses higher, the midnight streets emptier and more terrifying than in reality. To a child, inanimate objects have lives of their own: thus the smoke malevolently winds over Coketown like serpents and the pistons of the steam engines in the factory are "melancholy mad elephants."

The characters, too, are seen as children see people. Their peculiarities are heightened to eccentricities; their vices, to monstrous proportions. Most of the people in his novels are caricatures, characterized by their externals, almost totally predictable in behavior. We know little about them beyond their surface behavior; Dickens focuses on the outward man, not the inner motives. It is interesting to note, however, that Dickens was able to create intensely individual portraits even though he lacked the ability to analyze motivation and character developments. His characters are more than types or mere abstract representations of virtue or vice. They are intensely alive and thus memorable. The characters from a Dickens novel are remembered long after the plots and even the titles of the books have been forgotten.

DICKENS THE REFORMER

Dickens in his lifetime saw Great Britain change from a rural, agricultural "Merrie Old England" of inns, stagecoaches, and fox-hunting squires to an urbanized, commercial-industrial land of railroads, factories, slums, and a city proletariat. These changes are chronicled in his novels, and it is possible to read them as a social history of England. *Pickwick*, although set in 1827–28, reflects much of what still survived of the old eighteenth-century way of life. *Oliver Twist* (1837–39) shows the first impact of the Industrial Revolution - the poverty existing at that time and the feeble attempt to remedy it by workhouses. *Dombey and Son* (1846–48) describes the coming of the railroad, a symbol of change. Dombey, the merchant, sacrifices love, wife, and children for a position of power through money; yet he is already obsolete, for the industrialist is the ruler now.

Dickens grew increasingly bitter with each novel; his criticism of society became more radical, his **satire** more biting and less sweetened by humor. In his later novels he often broke out in indignant exasperation and almost hysterical anger. He figuratively mounted a soapbox, demanding that the "Lords and Gentlemen" do something about the appalling conditions of the poor.

In his early novels, society itself is not evil; it is only some people who are bad and who create misery for others by their callousness and neglect. By the time of *Dombey and Son* it is institutions which are evil, representing in that novel the self-expanding power of accumulated money. *Bleak House* (1852–53) attacks the law's delay and the self-perpetuating mass of futility it has become. *Hard Times* (1854) savagely lampoons the economic theories which Dickens considered responsible for much of human misery. The English historian, Lord Macaulay, charged that it was full of "sullen Socialism." *Of Little Dorritt* (1855–57), which attacks prisons and imprisonment for debt, George Bernard Shaw said that it was "more seditious than Karl Marx." In *Our Mutual Friend* (1864–65) we see the fully disillusioned Dickens. The atmosphere of the novel is grim, permeated with a sense of growing nightmare. There is the feeling that something deep and basic is wrong with the social order, something beyond the mere reforming of bad people or poorly-run institutions.

T. A. Jackson in *Charles Dickens: The Progress of a Radical* tries to claim him for the Marxists as a champion of the downtrodden masses. Yet Lenin, the father of Communist Russia, found Dickens intolerable in his "middle class sentimentality." George Orwell was probably correct when he stated that Dickens' criticism of society was neither political nor economic, but moral. Certainly Dickens offered no substitutes for the system or institutions he attacked. Thus in *A Tale of Two Cities* (1859) he expressed his loathing for the decadent French aristocracy of the ancient regime, but he seemed to like the triumphant democracy of the Revolution no better. In *Hard Times* he excoriates the exploitation of the industrial workers by the factory owners, but he is repelled almost equally by the attempt of the workers to form unions in self-defense. He seems to suggest that the Golden Rule is the only solution to class struggle.

BLEAK HOUSE

· ·

DICKENS AND BLEAK HOUSE

Bleak House was published as a book in 1853, when Dickens was at the height of his fame as a novelist. First published in serial parts (in shilling pamphlets) from March 1852, to September 1853, it is believed by many to contain his most impressive story. Although it lacks much of the humor of Dickens' early novels, *Bleak House* ranks high among his artistic achievements. In it Dickens not only satirized much of Victorian Society, but its theme of the law's delay is much more artistically unified with the diverse plot elements than are the plots and **themes** of his earlier novels. In addition, the preface to *Bleak House* ranks among the most interesting Dickens ever wrote. Here he defended the manner in which he disposed of one of the novel's characters (by spontaneous combustion), and made one of his rare statements on the nature of his art. "I have," he wrote, "purposely dwelt on the romantic side of familiar things."

Although the novel's plot is tightly organized, and all the incidents carefully related to the Chancery **theme**, the book is marred by its method of narration. Partly told by Esther

Summerson, and partly by Dickens as third-person narrator, the plot suffers somewhat from inconsistent changes of tense (Esther's narrative is told in the past tense although her activities are often concurrent with other parts of the story narrated by Dickens in the present tense), and by the fact that Esther is often out of character. Her astute observations and comments as to the worth of other characters are clearly Dickens speaking, not an inexperienced girl of twenty.

In addition to the inconsistencies of Esther's character, most of the other characters appear to be little more than sketchily drawn caricatures of real people. They are, in the usual Dickensian fashion, delineated by means of appropriate "tag lines," or characteristic actions. For example: Mr. Jarndyce's kindness is established by his constant reference to the "east wind", Matthew Bagnet, by his military manner; Mr. Tulkinghorn, by his silent watching; Lawrence Boythorn, by his explosive speech; and Harold Skimpole, by his "let Harold Skimpole live." Yet each appears to rise above Dickens' simple method of characterization to become a memorable individual whose character, or lack of it, is summed up by means of a kind of symbolic caricature. However, it must be remembered that although Dickens claimed to have "purposely dwelt on the romantic side of familiar things," many of the people and places that he wrote about were familiar because they were real.

Ranging over a great portion of Victorian Society, *Bleak House* represents Dickens' satiric comments on an inhuman, depersonalized legal system (Chancery, the police system represented by Mr. Bucket), false charity (Mrs. Jellby, Miss Pardiggle, Mr. Quale), political incompetence (the Noodles and Foodles), and conventional genteel respectability (Sir Leicester and Lady Dedlock). Each remains chained by the false sense of values to which he clings, and what solutions Dickens suggests, if indeed they can be called solutions, are revealed in the happiness and success achieved by those characters with whom both author and reader sympathize.

In spite of the complex difficulties of serial publication, *Bleak House* was as organized a novel as Dickens ever wrote. Using the Court of Chancery as a central symbol, the plot grows not as a consequence of invention, but as a consequence of a created image of the cumbersome structure of society with the idea of depth and surface. The Fashionable world of the Dedlocks and the inhuman legal system (represented by a number of greedy and depersonalized lawyers) are clearly related to the seething misery and crime of Tom - All Alone's and the grinding poverty of St. Albans through their common relationship in Chancery.

BRIEF SUMMARY OF THE PLOT

Ada Clare and Richard Carstone, wards in the famous Chancery suit of Jarndyce and Jarndyce, are offered refuge and help by the kindly master of Bleak House, John Jarndyce. Accompanying them to act as a companion to Ada and housekeeper of Bleak House is Esther Summerson, the novel's young and angelic heroine (who believes herself to be an orphan). The suit that has now been in Chancery through several generations of unfortunate Jarndyces is no closer to solution than ever. Indeed, the machinations of greedy lawyers and the inefficient and outmoded legal system have only made it more complex. (The suit thus serves as the focal point of the novel's **satire** against the Court of Chancery.)

As the plot develops, the romantic and good-natured Richard is drawn, like so many of his forebears, into the web of Chancery and gradually destroyed. Unable to succeed at a variety of endeavors (medicine, law, the army) because of his own weakness and because of the glittering promise of his inheritance in Chancery, Richard is crushed in spite of the efforts of Esther, John Jarndyce, and the love of the pure and unselfish Ada, all of whom fail to save him from the destruction that he tragically cannot help but pursue. Finally, at the novel's close, the suit is settled, but it is discovered that the estate has been entirely absorbed in legal costs (a final fiercely satiric comment on the failure of England's legal system).

Esther, who believes herself an orphan, is actually the daughter of Lady Dedlock, the wife of Sir Leicester Dedlock and a leader of fashionable society. Esther's father, Captain Hawdon, had been Lady Dedlock's lover prior to her marriage to Sir Leicester and because of that marriage, feeling that he had been deserted by Lady Dedlock (who actually believed he had been killed), assumed the identity of Mr. Nemo, a copyist of legal papers for Mr. Snagsby, a London law stationer. He finally died of malnutrition and drug addiction. When Lady Dedlock is surprised by the sudden appearance of the supposedly dead Captain Hawdon's handwriting on a legal document, Mr. Tulkinghorn, the Dedlock's lawyer, becomes curious. When Lady Dedlock seeks to find Captain Hawdon with the help of Jo, the crossing sweeper who leads her to Mr. Nemo's grave, the suspicious lawyer probes deeply into the secrets of her past. Finally, both Lady Dedlock and Mr. Tulkinghorn discover that the daughter whom Lady Dedlock had long believed dead (Esther) is alive and the lawyer confronts Lady Dedlock with his knowledge of her guilty secret.

Shortly thereafter, Mr. Tulkinghorn is murdered by Hortense, a French maid who had helped him to make his discoveries and whom Lady Dedlock had earlier discharged. Although at first George Rouncewell is accused of the murder by Inspector

Bucket, whom Sir Leicester has engaged; it is then discovered that Hortense is the guilty party. Unfortunately, Lady Dedlock's secret is revealed by others and she runs away to spare Sir Leicester the humiliation which such scandal is sure to bring. Although both Esther and Inspector Bucket pursue her diligently, bearing Sir Leicester's message of love and forgiveness, they fail to reach her in time and discover her dead on the steps of the cemetery where Captain Hawdon is buried.

At the same time that this story unfolds, Esther relates the story of her own proposals from the kindly Mr. Jarndyce and from Mr. Woodcourt, a young doctor who has befriended her. Released finally from her promise to Mr. Jarndyce to whom she owes so much, she finally marries Allan Woodcourt, and they settle down to an idyllic life in Yorkshire, where he has begun to practice as a doctor.

HISTORICAL BACKGROUND - POLITICAL, SOCIAL, AND ECONOMIC

From the multitude of political, social, and economic upheavals of the nineteenth century, four things emerge clearly. First: as a result of the passage of the various Reform Acts (1832, 1867, and 1884) that gradually extended the right of franchise (the vote) to greater numbers of Englishmen, as well as innumerable other parliamentary reforms, the English nation underwent a peaceful revolution from which has emerged modern British democracy. These changes were, of course, painfully slow, brought on in many cases by fear of revolt (following the American and French Revolutions at the close of the eighteenth century, the nineteenth witnessed revolts in Greece and Italy) and through the efforts of dedicated reformers like Jeremy Bentham, John Stuart Mill, William Cobbett, Robert Peel, and others.

Second: with the growth of democracy through the franchise and as a result of social unrest fostered by rising industrialism, England awoke to the fact that great numbers of people had become victims of industrial slavery. It thus became the purpose of reformers (and authors like Dickens) to free this new class of slaves (legal slavery had been prohibited in England since 1833). In addition, there arose a recognition for the need of religious tolerance and of universal education if the new democracy was to be permanent and successful. To these ends, it was the purpose of the following acts of Parliament to free this new class of industrial slave and to promote religious tolerance, a purpose which has remained a primary principle of government to the present day: Ashley's Factory Act (1844); Jews Eligible for Municipal Office (1845); Ashley's Act for ten-hour day (1847); Catholic Emancipation Act (1850); Property Qualification for Parliament Abolished (1858); Parliament Opened to Jews (1858); Franchise for Settled Workmen (1869); Abolition of Imprisonment for Debt (1869); The Elementary Education Act (1870); Employer's Liability Act (1800).

Third: the nineteenth century was an age of imperialist expansion. As in the Elizabethan Age (which began with the defeat of the Spanish Armada in 1588), England emerged as not only a great industrial nation, but a great military and colonial power as well. The century saw England's involvement in the Crimean War (1854–56), The Sepoy Mutiny in India (1857–60), and the Boer War (1899–1902); and as a result Queen Victoria became Empress of India and the British Empire became the largest that the world had ever known. (The breaking up of that Empire began gradually after World War I and, of course, was greatly accelerated after World War II.)

Fourth: it was a century of scientific progress. In addition to the advances in medicine by men like Louis Pasteur and

Robert Koch, there were the advances in natural science by men like Charles Darwin (*Origin of the Species*, 1859), and Thomas Henry Huxley (popularizer of Darwin and biologist). Along with these advances came great changes in communications and transportation (the telephone, telegraph, and railway) and the application of steam to manufacturing (the power loom, the spinning jenny, and the cotton gin).

BLEAK HOUSE

. . . .

CHAPTER ONE: IN CHANCERY

It is a foggy London afternoon early in November. The air is heavy with soot and the roadways are clogged with mud and grime. "The afternoon is rawest, and the fog densest, and the muddy streets muddiest" at the Temple Bar, Lincoln's Inn Hall. For here the Lord High Chancellor sits at the bench in the High Court of Chancery.

Like the fog and the mud of the ancient London streets, the Court of Chancery moves through its business without direction and without movement. It seems as if the fog has penetrated even the courtroom itself, for around the Chancellor's bench it hangs heavy. Before him hangs an unlit lantern at which he gazes sightlessly. Justice is not only blind, but the pathway to justice is obscure.

Below the Chancellor sit the lesser members of the court. There sits the registrar who calls the cases before the bar. Beneath the registrar are the advocates and the solicitors who represent the innumerable petitioners whose cases the court is to decide. Below the bench occupied by the solicitors are the shorthand writers, court reporters, and newspapermen. Today the newsmen are noticeably absent because the case before the court is Jarndyce and Jarndyce, a case so ancient as to be no longer news-worthy. Around the courtroom stand the regulars, the hopeless petitioners, and spectators.

The Court of Chancery, like the weather, is mired in the mud of legal red tape. Nor are common sense and justice able to penetrate the fog which surrounds the court's procedures. Cases here almost never come to a solution. Instead, they drag on endlessly until the plaintiff and defendant alike are destroyed by the ever-mounting court costs.

The case before the court this afternoon, Jarndyce and Jarndyce, has become so complicated with the passage of time that "no man alive knows what it means." It has long become a joke among members of the legal profession, many of whom have been brought upon it. Among them, and appearing before the court this afternoon, is Mr. Tangle. It is said of Mr. Tangle, that except for Jarndyce and Jarndyce, he has "never read anything else since he left school."

Among the early victims of the case, we are told, was Tom Jarndyce, who long ago "blew his brains out at a coffee house in Chancery Lane." At present, Mr. Tangle is representing a distant cousin now a party to the suit. Mr. Tangle has brought before the court two of the many wards of the court in the case, and they are waiting in the Chancellor's private chambers. Many previous wards have been born, grown old, and died. Now the procedure is to be repeated, for the end of the case is no closer to solution than ever.

There are two other spectators in the courtroom who are identified only as the man from Shropshire and the mad old lady who carries in a net bag her legal papers, "consisting of paper matches and dry lavender." Like so many others, neither of these unfortunates has ever been able to engage the court's attention.

Finally, at the moment when the wheels of justice seem to grind, though exceedingly slowly, Mr. Tangle interrupts. He reminds the Lord Chancellor that the wards in the case of Jarndyce and Jarndyce await him in his chambers. Almost immediately the court is adjourned and the Lord Chancellor retires to his chambers to assign the wards of the court into the keeping of their cousin.

As usual the day has passed and nothing has happened. Cases have been postponed, petitioners have been avoided, and everyone vanishes from the courtroom.

Comment

The chapter appropriately serves to introduce to the reader the Court of Chancery which serves as the motivating force for much of the action of the novel. Dickens, who had himself served as a shorthand reporter in his youth, and who had recently been involved in a number of Chancery suits, accurately records the inefficiency and injustice of that institution. The way is prepared for the introduction of the major characters in the next chapter. Several minor characters, whose stories will be told later in great detail, are introduced and help to arouse the reader's curiosity.

Introduced also in the chapter are those somber symbols (mud and fog) and their counterpart (the court and its procedures) which set the tone of the novel and limit its action. Note too, Dickens' characteristic use of descriptive names and "tag lines" which help to identify his characters. We meet, for example, Mr. Tangle, whose name describes his part in the legal proceedings and whose constant address to the Lord Chancellor of "Mlud" is a play on the word mud, as well as representative of the form of shorthand usually employed by those who write legal documents.

CHAPTER TWO: IN FASHION

"Both the world of fashion and the Court of Chancery are things of precedent and usage, oversleeping Rip Van Winkles." And so, deftly Dickens compares one little world with another: the unreal world of the courtroom which so influences the lives which it touches, with the world of fashionable people. This, too, is a world made up of people like the Lord High Chancellor who are unaware of the larger world about them. It is a little world ruled by Lady Dedlock, the "high priestess of fashion," whose every movement, dress, conversation, and boredom are copied by those to whom appearances are important.

Lady Dedlock has just returned to London from the Dedlock "place" in Lincolnshire, Chesney Wold, a place damp, moldy, and dreary. She is, at the moment, preparing for a trip to Paris where she intends to spend a few weeks - a fact of much interest to her devoted followers. A woman attractive and elegant, Lady

Dedlock is some twenty years younger than her husband, Sir Leicester Dedlock, who is said to have married her for love.

Sir Leicester Dedlock, the latest baronet of that line, is a man over sixty-seven with a "twist of the gout." A ceremonious and stately man, he is known for his gallantry to Lady Dedlock. Like all of the Dedlocks before him, he is an "honorable, obstinate, truthful, high-spirited, intensely prejudiced, perfectly unreasonable man." These two, then, are the last of the Dedlocks, for they have no children.

Among the visitors to the Dedlock's town house is Mr. Tulkinghorn, the family lawyer. He is a man "rusty" and secretive, who seems surrounded by the confidence of those whom he advises. Dressed all in black, as becomes a man without feelings or vices, Mr. Tulkinghorn has brought some legal papers which have to do with Lady Dedlock's interest in the case of Jarndyce and Jarndyce. As he reads to the bored Dedlocks from the documents prepared by his copyist, Lady Dedlock casually glances at the handwriting on the documents. Suddenly she becomes violently agitated and faints. Lord Leicester, believing his wife affected by the bad weather, helps her to her room.

Comment

In this chapter Dickens uses another plot device which serves to engage the reader's attention and hint at things to come. This device is called **foreshadowing**. When Lady Dedlock becomes so violently agitated by the handwriting on the affidavits which Mr. Tulkingtorn has brought, the reader becomes aware that her involvement in Jarndyce and Jarndyce is greater than she admits.

The lawyer, the papers concerning Jarndyce and Jarndyce, and Lady Dedlock's interest in the case, bring together immediately what seem to be totally different plot strands. If we remember that *Bleak House* was first published in twenty serial parts, we realize that this was a familiar device of Dickens' to rouse the reader's interest and to whet his appetite for the parts yet to come.

CHAPTER THREE: A PROGRESS

(Esther Summerson narrates her own story.)

"I can remember, when I was a little girl indeed, I used to say to my doll when we were alone together, 'Now Dolly, I am not clever, you know very well, and you must be patient with me, like a dear.'"

Beginning then with the memories of her earliest years, Esther relates her strange history. As a child she had lived with her godmother, a strange and puritanical woman, who kept secret Esther's parentage, except for a few veiled hints. The result was that Esther's childhood was lonely and withdrawn, and the only companion to whom she could talk was her doll. Although she attended the local school as a day boarder, she was never able to form any fast friendships there. The close up-bringing of her godmother and the fact that she was much younger than the other girls prevented that. Indeed, while the other little girls at the school celebrated their birthdays with parties at school, Esther complained there were "none on mine."

Thus, with the secret of her birth held fast by her godmother and a servant, Mrs. Rachel, Esther's life proceeded with the same monotonous regularity. When she attempts to question

Mrs. Rachel on the subject of her parentage, she is greeted with a brusque "Goodnight, Esther." She is informed only that there is some disgrace attached to her birth, a disgrace which she will have to bear through a life of self-denial and repentance.

An affectionate and curious child, Esther lives under this arrangement until she is fourteen. It is interrupted only once, by the appearance of a strange visitor to whom Esther is introduced as "the child," and bade return to her room. Finally, her godmother, visibly affected by the strain of caring for Esther and the secret she kept, dies suddenly. Again the stranger appears to Esther and introduces himself as Mr. Kenge of Kenge and Carboys, solicitors. Inadvertently he reveals to Esther that the woman she had called godmother was in reality her aunt. As he explained smoothly, "Aunt in fact, if not in law."

Mr. Kenge (called by the members of his profession "Conversation" Kenge) then reveals to Esther the details of an offer which he had made to Esther's godmother, two years earlier, concerning Esther's future. A Mr. Jarndyce, his client, had offered to bear the expenses of Esther's education. "Her reasonable wants shall be anticipated," and she will be sent to school "where she shall be eminently qualified to discharge her duty in that station of life into which ... it has pleased Providence to call her." Overwhelmed and surprised, Esther quickly accepts the offer. Gathering her few belongings, with the exception of her doll, which she buried in the garden, she bids Mrs. Rachel goodbye and tearfully leaves the only home she has ever known. After a brief journey by coach, she arrives at Greenleaf School in Reading, where she is greeted by one of the twin Miss Donnys, managers of the school.

Esther's six years at Greenleaf are happy ones. Feeling that she had somehow failed her godmother, Esther determines "to do good to someone." As a result, her birthday annually brought "so many tokens of affectionate remembrance that my room was beautiful with them from New Year's Day to Christmas."

When she is twenty, Esther receives a letter from Kenge and Carboys which informs her that she is now ready to be received into the home of Mr. Jarndyce, who, having been awarded custody of the wards in that famous case, desires her services as a companion to one of the wards.

Five days later, after a parting filled with tears and good wishes from the Misses Donny and the girls at the school, Esther leaves by stage.

Arriving at the London offices of Kenge and Carboys, she is conducted to the Court of Chancery, where she is introduced to the wards in the case: Ada Clare and her cousin, Richard Carstone. They are then ushered into the presence of the Lord High Chancellor, who approves of the arrangements thus made, and they are dismissed.

After leaving the Chancery building, the three soon become fast friends. They are shortly troubled, however by a meeting with a strange little old lady carrying a little bag filled with her "documents" who is happy to have the "honor" of meeting the wards in the Jarndyce case.

Comment

Although Dickens narrates the chapter through the person of Esther Summerson, he still retains something of authorial control. Her narrative is much more detailed, observant, than would either be likely or possible for a young girl as innocent and inexperienced as she. For example, when Ada is presented to the Lord High Chancellor, Esther notes that he "at his best, appeared so poor a substitute for the love and pride of parents." Related as a first person narrative in the past tense, the chapter has the immediacy of autobiography. Although, from time to time, Dickens will return as omniscient author, more than half the story is told by Esther herself.

This chapter also introduces a device familiar in not only the nineteenth century novel, but in melodrama - the device of coincidence. In this case, the first of many chance meetings that will occur among characters already introduced in other chapters is used. Here, however, it is managed very well. The mad old lady of the Chancery Court might well have accidentally met the Jarndyce wards.

Chapter Three is, of course, like Chapters One and Two, merely introductory, serving only as a means of setting the stage for the story which is to follow.

CHAPTER FOUR: TELESCOPIC PHILANTHROPY

Leaving the Chancery Court, Ada, Richard, and Esther are informed by Mr. Kenge that they are to spend the night at the home of a Mrs. Jellyby, a lady "who is much sought after by philanthropists." Confessing total ignorance of that famous lady, they are then conducted to her home by Mr. William Guppy, a minor clerk in Mr. Kenge's office. After a brief trip through the twisting, narrow, and foggy London streets, they arrive at her home, which is a dirty, disorganized establishment, filled with neglected, unhealthy-looking children. Mrs. Jellyby herself is "a pretty, plump woman, of from forty to fifty, with handsome eyes, although they had a curious habit of seeming to look a long way off."

Philanthropy is Mrs. Jellyby's passion, a passion at the present "devoted to the subject of Africa; with a view to the general cultivation of the coffee berry - and the natives." Unfortunately, it is obvious that Mrs. Jellyby's passion for reform and good works does not extend either to her own children or to her appearance. We are told, for example, that she is a woman "who had good hair, but was much too occupied with her African duties to brush it." One could not help but notice that "her dress didn't nearly meet up the back."

Among the Jellyby children introduced to the reader are a rather ragged and dirty little boy who had caught his head between the iron railings; Caddy, Mrs. Jellyby's eldest daughter, "an unhealthy, though by no means plain girl," who acts as her mother's unwilling secretary in the endless correspondence of her African affairs, and finally, Peepy, another unkempt and dirty little boy who manages to fall down a flight of stairs in front of the visitors. It is an event that does not, however, raise any anxiety in his mother, though it horrifies her visitors.

As Richard, Ada, and Esther listen to Mrs. Jellyby's enthusiastic, if puzzling, explanation of her African interests, Esther comforts the bruised Peepy. When she, Ada, and Richard return to their rooms before dinner to freshen up, Esther takes him with her and allows him to sleep in her bed while she entertains the numerous other little Jellybys with the story of Little Red Riding Hood.

The rooms that the visitors are to occupy are much like the rest of the house. The doors will not lock, there is no hot water, and the pitchers from which such water might be poured have no handles. So Richard, Ada, and Esther dress quickly and hurry to the warmth of the drawing-room fire.

Soon after seven o'clock, they all go down to dinner where they are introduced to a "mild, bald-headed gentleman," who turns out to be Mr. Jellyby, and to Mr. Quale, a man "with large shining knobs for temples" who, like Mrs. Jellyby, is a philanthropist. During dinner, Mr. Quale and Mrs. Jellyby engage in an involved discussion about the brotherhood of humanity. Mr. Jellyby, although many times on the verge of saying something, never does. Meanwhile, Esther and Ada quietly sit in a corner and entertain the Jellyby children with the story of Puss in Boots as Richard, confused and mute, sits next to Mr. Jellyby and listens to Mrs. Jellyby and Mr. Quale.

It is nearly midnight before Esther, Ada, and Richard are able to get to bed. There, as Ada sleeps, Esther is surprised by a visit from Caddy, ink-stained and tearful. Ashamed of her family and home, Caddy pours out her heart and at last falls asleep kneeling at Esther's feet, and Esther with Caddy's head in her lap sleeps fitfully.

Comment

Dickens varies his attacks on the institutions and society of his age with his satiric presentation of Mrs. Jellyby and Mr. Quale. Like numerous other charitable persons and institutions in Victorian England, they work unceasingly to relieve poverty and misery in the far corners of the world while ignoring the suffering in their midst.

For example, the Evangelical wing of the Church of England had earlier fought to end the slave trade and had succeeded in doing so by 1807. However, at home, they believed in the economic theory of laissez faire and resisted all attempts at Parliamentary reforms that might have succeeded in relieving the widespread poverty of the English working classes.

Even the various reform bills did little to improve the economic conditions of the poor, so that progress toward better distribution of England's great industrial wealth was not achieved to any serious degree until the beginning of the twentieth century.

CHAPTER FIVE: A MORNING ADVENTURE

The next morning is raw and the fog still heavy, but Ada, Richard, and Esther, curious about London, go for a walk before breakfast, accompanied by Caddy. Having been informed by Caddy that "Ma won't be down for ever so long," they walk without direction through the busy London streets. As Caddy confides to Esther the difficulties of her life, they walk, noticing the "varieties of streets, the quantity of people going to and fro, the number of vehicles passing and repassing ... the extra-ordinary creatures in rags, secretly groping among the swept out rubbish." Thus engaged, they unexpectedly find themselves in front of the Court of Chancery, where they are again greeted by Miss Flite, the little old lady whom they had met the day before.

Greeting the wards in the Jarndyce case, as she did a day earlier, the mad old lady explains that she often spends the hours before the court opens in her "garden." Thinking their meeting again so soon to be a good omen for settlement of her own "case" in Chancery, she invites Ada, Richard, Esther, and

Caddy to visit her rooms, and they, not knowing how to excuse themselves and half-curious, accompany her to a nearby narrow street, where she points to a shop bearing a sign which read,

KROOK, RAG, AND BOTTLE WAREHOUSE DEALERS IN MARINE STORES

Through the window of the shop they are able to see the most amazing collection of items, dirty bottles of all kinds: "blacking bottles, medicine bottles, ginger beer, and soda-water bottles, pickle bottles, wine bottles, ink...." There are "heaps of old crackled parchment scrolls, and discolored and dogs-eared law papers," and among the litter of rags and bric-a-brac a pile of bones can be seen. As Richard remarks good-humoredly, "picked very clean" like "the bones of clients."

As the little group waits outside the shop, peering into its dark and gloomy interior, a short, withered old man comes to the door and inquires if they have anything to sell. The old lady, still searching for the key to her door, introduces the strange little man as her landlord, Krook, whose shop was called by the neighbors, the Court of Chancery and he the Lord High Chancellor.

Like the Court of Chancery, Krook's shop has never been cleaned, nor has any part of its stock ever been removed. Instead, more and more is continually added to an already considerable heap, piled haphazardly in dusty, dirty mounds. Like the Lord High Chancellor, Krook has never changed his method of business, nor has he ever cleaned the shop.

Upon learning that his visitors are wards in Jarndyce and Jarndyce, Krook relates the story of poor Tom Jarndyce, to whom he had talked on the morning of his suicide, and shows a surprising knowledge of the case. As they listen, "Ada's color had entirely left her and Richard was scarcely less pale."

Finally, as they are ushered into Miss Flite's room, she explains "her landlord was a little m-." The room is large and sparsely furnished, containing only the bare necessities of existence and a half-dozen work bags containing "documents." In the curtained-off section of the room she shows her visitors a number of canaries with names like Hope, Youth, and Beauty. They do not often get the chance to sing because they have to be protected from Mr. Krook's cat, Lady Jane.

On the way downstairs, the old lady points to a door on the second floor and whispers that the only other lodger who lives there is a scrivener, rumored by the children of the neighborhood to have sold himself to the devil. In the shop again, they meet Mr. Krook who is filling a well in the floor with quantities of waste paper. Although they are informed by Mr. Krook that he cannot read or write, he traces upon a wall the words, Jarndyce and Bleak House, explaining that he had learned to copy from the many legal documents in his possession.

As they return to Mrs. Jellyby's, Richard and Ada are disheartened. Having met at every turn some reminder of the sad case in which they are innocently involved, they determine not to be changed by it. The next afternoon, after saying goodbye to Mrs. Jellyby and Caddy, they depart by carriage for Bleak House.

Comment

Dickens continues to reinforce his attack on the Chancery through the use of symbols. As the shop of Mr. Krook is representative of the Chancery Court and its ways, so the old lady's birds are symbolically the many innocents involved in the Chancery's procedures. Like the birds, they are caged and will never see freedom. Instead they are the prey of unscrupulous lawyers and outmoded methods which in no small degree resemble Mr. Krook's hungry cat.

These symbols, of course, also serve to unify the various portions of the novel's plot, which is developed in several directions at once and which involves many different types of characters.

CHAPTER SIX: QUITE AT HOME

As the carriage containing Esther, Ada, and Richard nears Bleak House, it is met by a messenger sent by John Jarndyce, master of the house, who bids them welcome in similar notes, couched in friendly terms.

Finally, arriving at Bleak House, they discover him to be a hearty, robust man with iron-grey hair and a pleasant expression in his eyes. Nearly sixty years of age, he is a modest man who can neither bear to discuss anything unpleasant nor receive profuse thanks for any kindness that he has performed.

Bleak House is one of those "delightfully irregular" old houses with many rooms, halls, and passageways. Reflecting its owner, who takes them happily through the house, it is a pleasant place, filled with interesting furniture, portraits, and a hospitable warmth.

After the tour of the house, Esther is presented by a maid with the keys to the household, and she prepares to assume her duties as the housekeeper of Bleak House as well as companion to Ada.

At dinner, Esther, Richard, and Ada are introduced to another of Mr. Jarndyce's guests, Mr. Harold Skimpole. Mr. Skimpole is a rather helpless and impractical man who has "perhaps a dozen" children, but has remained a child himself. Although Mr. Skimpole was educated for the medical profession, it is soon apparent that he is a failure at it, as at everything else.

He is a man whose wants were few. As he explains, "give him papers, conversation, music, mutton, coffee, landscape ... and a little claret, and he asked no more." His only demand upon the world is "let Harold Skimpole live." And live he does, on the generosity of such friends as Mr. Jarndyce and others, who are thereby accorded the privilege of "enjoying the luxury of generosity."

Richard and Esther are admitted to that great company of Mr. Skimpole's providers that evening, when he informs them that he is about to be arrested for debt. Feeling he must develop generosity in new soil, "he imposed upon them to provide "twenty-four pounds sixteen and seven-pence ha' penny."

Mr. Jarndyce, apparently informed by one of the servants of what has happened, reproaches them good-humoredly, and secures a promise from them not to become involved in Mr. Skimpole's "offers" again. He does not, however, in any manner reproach the "childlike" Skimpole, explaining "you can't make him responsible. The idea of Harold Skimpole with design, or plan, or knowledge of consequence! Ha ha ha."

Comment

Although Harold Skimpole was intended as a characterization of the poet, Leigh Hunt, he emerges almost immediately in the novel as a despicable parasite.

Among the many unifying devices or symbols which Dickens uses in *Bleak House*, his use of variation in the weather as a **foreshadowing** may be clearly seen. For example, as Esther, Ada, and Richard leave the distorted world of the Jellybys and of Krook's Bottle Shop, the weather is foggy and damp. As they approach Bleak House, it brightens and the day becomes pleasant.

Even characters are often described in terms of the weather. John Jarndyce's reference to the East Wind as an ill-omen which brings on his rheumatism is a protective device behind which he hides his generous nature. He prefers the gentler winds from other quarters which bring fair weather.

CHAPTER SEVEN: THE GHOSTS' WALK

At the Dedlock place in Lincolnshire the rain continues to fall. "It has rained so long and hard that Mrs. Rouncewell, the old housekeeper at Chesney Wold, has several times taken off her spectacles and cleaned them, to make certain that the drops were not on the glasses." In charge, now that the Dedlocks are in Paris, Mrs. Rouncewell has been at Chesney Wold for more than fifty years as the trusted servant of the Dedlocks. Indeed, it is said that when Sir Leicester Dedlock comes home he shakes hands with her.

Although she is an ideal servant who always knows her place, her life has not been without its difficulties. She has had two sons, each of whom has brought her some grief and embarrassment. George, the younger, had years before run off to the army and had never been heard from since, while the elder was sent away from Chesney Wold at the request of SiroLeicester because he was mechanically inclined and inventive, both qualities which frightened the aristocratic and conservative Sir Leicester.

Visiting Mrs. Rouncewell this morning is her grandson, Watt. Although he is the son of her elder, and like him in that he is "just out of apprenticeship," a mechanical sort, he reminds her of her lost son, George. As they talk, Watt is attracted to Rosa, a pretty girl from the village who is being trained by his grandmother as a maid. As he questions his grandmother on the subject of Rosa, they are interrupted by the arrival of two strangers from London. The strangers are Mr. William Guppy, whom we have met before at the office of Kenge and Carboys, and a friend. They have been attending a magistrate's meeting nearby and wishing to see Chesney Wold, explain to Mrs. Rouncewell that they are lawyers acquainted with Mr. Tulkinghorn. Although the Dedlocks are not at home, the name of Mr. Tulkinghorn produces the desired result, and Mrs. Rouncewell makes them welcome.

Mr. Guppy and friend, exhausted after a tour of Chesney Wold where they have looked upon a seemingly endless series of Dedlock portraits, enter the drawing room. Mr. Guppy is immediately attracted to a portrait over the fireplace which Rouncewell identifies as the present Lady Dedlock. Although he cannot account for his feeling of familiarity with the figure in the portrait, Mr. Guppy feels strongly that he has seen it, or Lady Dedlock, somewhere before.

When Mr. Guppy and friend leave, Watt and Rosa return, and Mrs. Rouncewell recounts to them the story of Chesney Wold's famous Ghost Walk. "In the wicked days of Charles the First - I mean, of course, in the wicked days of the rebels," Sir Morbury Dedlock had allied himself with that unfortunate King, and it was rumored that his lady had favored the rebel cause. As a result the lady led a troubled life which finally ended in a serious injury reportedly received in the act of crippling one of the Dedlock horses so it could not be used in the King's cause. From that time forward, she walked only with the aid of the stone balustrade on the terrace, but with greater difficulty every day. Finally, she fell one day upon the pavement, and Sir Morbury rushed to her side. As he tried to raise her, she spoke to him in the only words she had uttered to him since her injury. "I will die here where I walked…. I will walk here, until the pride of his house is humbled. And when calamity, or when disgrace is coming to it, let the Dedlocks listen for my step."

Even as they talk with Watt, Rosa and Mrs. Rouncewell imagine that they can hear footsteps on the terrace.

Comment

Again Dickens uses the device of **foreshadowing**. In this case it is two-fold. First, the continuing bad weather indicates the coming of some evil event to Chesney Wold, and now the story of the family curse adds to that likely event.

The Puritan Revolt (1642–1649) was led by Oliver Cromwell, leader of the "Roundheads." The cavaliers under Charles I were finally defeated in 1645, and Charles himself was beheaded in 1649. After the death of Oliver Cromwell in 1658, his son Richard was not strong enough to retain control, and the Puritan Parliament was dissolved. The Stuart King Charles II, son of the executed Charles I, was recalled from exile in France and assumed the throne in 1660.

BLEAK HOUSE

TEXTUAL ANALYSIS

CHAPTERS 8-15

. . . .

CHAPTER EIGHT: COVERING A MULTITUDE OF SINS

Esther, having assumed her duties as housekeeper, is one day interrupted by Mr. Jarndyce as she attends to her appropriate task. He takes her to a small room next to his bedchamber that he refers to as his Growlery, a place where he retires to growl when he is out of humor. Here he takes her into his confidence and explains the story of Jarndyce and Jarndyce.

"A certain Jarndyce, in an evil hour, made a great fortune, and made a great Will." Although the will itself was made a long time ago, the effect of the trusts made in that will are still felt by its heirs. Among those heirs to the will was Mr. Jarndyce's uncle, "poor Tom Jarndyce," who had taken the case too seriously. In spite of the fact that the will has been in Chancery for many years, the case is no closer to a solution than ever. Instead, the legal squabbles and disputes continue to consume the estate in endless legal fees and "cartloads of legal papers."

Years before, when Tom Jarndyce had lived at Bleak House, the house had been called the Peak. He had shut it up and given it the name of Bleak House while he poured "over the wicked heaps of papers in the suit hoping against hope," to bring it to a close. And "in the meanwhile the place became dilapidated, the wind whistled through the cracked walls. The rain fell through the cracked walls. The rain fell through the broken roof." Like another Jarndyce property in London, Bleak House has fallen into ruin. It has, however, been redeemed from the fate of the London place, by the coming of John Jarndyce. These, then, are the only tangible results of the suit that has lasted so long. Nor is it likely that any improvement will be made in the foreseeable future, since the legal system that had created such conditions still exists. According to John Jarndyce, wherever the Great Seal of Chancery appears, ruin and decay are sure to follow. "These are the Great Seal's impressions - all over England - the children know them."

Mr. Jarndyce feels better after having told Esther these facts that have been so long on his mind. When he has finished his tale in the Growlery, he offers to give Esther any information which he might supply about her. Esther, however, declines his kind offer, feeling certain that Mr. Jarndyce will tell her anything she ought to know. Much pleased by her confidence, Mr. Jarndyce then turns his thoughts to finding of a suitable profession for Richard.

So many persons both in and out of the neighborhood know of John Jarndyce that it seems to Esther they all want something from him. Would-be philanthropists of all sorts besiege him with cards and letters asking for contributions. They ask for rags, for clothing, for soup, for autographs, for money - in short, for everything. Among the most persistent of his besiegers is Mrs. Pardiggle, "who was nearly as powerful a correspondent as Mrs. Jellyby herself." Mr. Jarndyce, himself, remarks, "There were two classes of charitable people; one, the people who did little and made a great deal of noise; the other, the people who did a great deal and made no noise at all." Mrs. Pardiggle belonged to the former class and Mr. Jarndyce to the latter.

One day, while Esther and Ada are alone, Mrs. Pardiggle honors Bleak House with a personal visit. With her she has her five sons, each of whom is an unwilling contributor to one or another of her charities. Indeed, "the face of each child darkened, as the amount of his contribution was mentioned." Alfred, the youngest (five) has been already pledged "never through life to use tobacco in any form."

The present object of Mrs. Pardiggle's charity is the family of a brickmaker, whose poverty-striken home is visited among those on "her rounds." Here, the determined Mrs. Pardiggle distributes religious tracts and preaches to the antagonistic family as Ada and Esther attempt to comfort Jenny, the brickmaker's wife, whose baby has just died in her arms. Later, they return to the cottage, and, assisted by a kindly neighbor of the brickmaker, comfort poor Jenny.

Comment

The attack upon charitable institutions becomes more specific through the introduction of Mrs. Pardiggle. Like many philanthropists, she attempts to alleviate the misery of the poor without any real understanding of the problems which confront them. Instead of attending to their immediate physical needs, she attempts to reform them by preaching and handling out religious tracts.

CHAPTER NINE: SIGNS AND TOKENS

Esther, Ada, and Richard pass the winter pleasantly. Each day they grow more fond of one another, and as Esther senses, Richard's feelings show more than fondness for Ada. Unfortunately, Richard has not settled on the choice of a profession. Although he has for a time considered being a sailor, nothing comes of it. Even though Mr. Jarndyce has written to Sir Leicester Dedlock for his help, the baronet has only replied, "that he would be happy to advance the prospects of the young gentleman if it should ever prove to be in his power, which was not at all probable."

One morning at breakfast a letter arrives announcing the visit from a Mr. Boythorn, an old schoolfellow of Mr. Jarndyce. When he arrives shortly thereafter, he turns out to be, as Mr. Jarndyce had described him, a hearty, impetuous, noisy fellow. He is ten years older than Mr. Jarndyce but he gives the impression of being some years younger. Active and energetic, he is given to speaking only in superlatives. He is, in Mr. Jarndyce's words, "a tremendous fellow."

At the moment much of Mr. Boythorn's energy seems to be engaged in a legal dispute with a Lincolnshire neighbor, Sir Leicester Dedlock. Each claims the right of way to a "green pathway" which Sir Leicester has decided to close up. Mr. Boythorn, of course, reacts with customary violence. When Sir Leicester has the pathway barricaded, Mr. Boythorn chops it up for firewood. When Sir Leicester sends men to construct another, Mr. Boythorn peppers them with split peas and soaks them with a fire hose. And so the dispute continues, now in court.

The next morning a letter arrives from Kenge and Carboys, who are representing Mr. Boythorn in the matter of the pathway, advising him that their representative would shortly arrive.

That representative, of course, is Mr. Guppy. He has an entirely new suit of glossy clothes on, a shining hat, lilac kid gloves … "besides which, he quite scented the dining room with bear's-grease and other perfumery."

Following a difficult conference with Mr. Boythorn, whom he called a "tartar," Mr. Guppy surprises Esther with a proposal of marriage. Although he pleads mightily, admitting that his suit is a poor one. Esther refuses as kindly as she can in the circumstances. Later when she is alone upstairs she tells us, "I was surprised myself by beginning to laugh about it, and then surprised myself still more by beginning to cry."

Comment

A new complication is introduced into the plot. The great diversity of characters introduced in preceding chapters is drawn closer together by their mutual involvement in various legal actions. For example, Sir Leicester, Ada, and Richard are petitioners in the suit of Jarndyce and Jarndyce. Now Mr. Boythorn is involved in an action against Sir Leicester.

Again Dicken's device of descriptive name is used. The character of Boythorn is revealed in his name. He is both a "boyish" and "thorny" man, full of life and difficult to deal with.

CHAPTER TEN: THE LAW-WRITER

The shop of Mr. Snagsby, law stationer, is located on the eastern border of Chancery Lane. It is a shop filled with legal forms, stamps, quill pens, red tape, pocketbooks, inkstands, and all manner of devices employed by the legal profession. Here

Mr. Snagsby, "a mild, bald, timid man" lives with his wife and a young servant called Guster (short for Augusta). Mrs. Snagsby, a violent, shrewish woman, rules both Mr. Snagsby and Guster with an iron hand.

Across Chancery Lane in Lincoln's Inn Fields is the house of Mr. Tulkinghorn, solicitor to the Dedlocks. Here, surrounded by old law books and locked cabinets, he sits alone this afternoon, playing with bits of red and black sealing wax, as he debates something which is on his mind. Around six o'clock, Mr. Tulkinghorn suddenly arranges the bits of wax, takes his hat, and leaves for Mr. Snagsby's stationery shop.

Informed by Guster of Mr. Tulkinghorn's presence, Mr. Snagsby comes down into the shop still eating his dinner. Here he is questioned by Mr. Tulkinghorn about some legal documents recently copied for the stationer. After looking at his record book under Jarndyce and Jarndyce, Mr. Snagsby informs Mr. Tulkinghorn that the documents in question were copied by a law-writer named Nemo, who lived across the Lane over Krook's Bottle Shop. Struck by the fact that Nemo is Latin for no one, Mr. Tulkinghorn is escorted to the bottle shop by Mr. Snagsby. He then gets rid of Mr. Snagsby by telling him that he is not going in, but has another engagement. When Snagsby leaves, Mr. Tulkinghorn returns to the shop and asks Mr. Krook about his boarder.

Providing a candle, Mr. Krook escorts Mr. Tulkinghorn to the second floor, where they discover Nemo, ragged and unshaven, lying open-eyed in the dark and dirty room. In the air "through the general sickness and faintness, and the odor of stale tobacco, there comes into the lawyer's mouth the bitter, vapid taste of opium." Although they call and knock repeatedly, the reclining Nemo does not answer.

Comment

Again Dickens employs symbol as a means of revealing character. Mr. Tulkinghorn is described as a crow - a black and solitary bird.

CHAPTER ELEVEN: OUR DEAR BROTHER

After relighting the candle, which had gone out Mr. Tulkinghorn and Mr. Krook become aware that Nemo is dead. Mr. Krook calls excitedly for Miss Flite, his other lodger, to fetch a doctor. The doctor, who recognizes Nemo as a man who "has purchased opium off me for the past year and a half," quietly pronounces Nemo dead of an overdose of opium. Mr. Tulkinghorn then advises Mr. Krook that further information concerning the dead man might be had from Mr. Snagsby, who had employed Nemo as a law writer.

Unfortunately, Mr. Snagsby is unable to provide any information beyond the fact that Nemo had come into his shop a year and a half before, seeking work as a law writer, in which capacity he had employed him. Since Mr. Snagsby is thus unable to provide the desired information, Mr. Tulkinghorn suggests to Mr. Krook that they search the dead man's portmanteau, an object which had earlier attracted the interest of each. When the search of that article fails to produce anything beyond "some worthless articles of clothing," a "bundle of pawnbroker's duplicates," and "a few scraps of newspaper all referring to Coroner's Inquest," they decide to send for the beadle. Since there is obviously nothing more to be learned at present, Mr. Tulkinghorn returns to his home.

The beadle circulates through the neighborhood, already buzzing with the news of the strange event, seeking witnesses for the Coroner's Jury. Although he tries earnestly and officiously, there are no witnesses available.

The next morning, at the appointed hour, the members of the Coroner's Jury anxiously await the arrival of the Coroner in the Sol's Arms, a public house often frequented by the Coroner in his unofficial capacity. Outside a crowd of curious neighbors waits. Since early in the day, they have sustained themselves with frequent visits to the Sol's Arms bar and the children in the crowd have recourse to the pieman on the corner. As they are being entertained by a local "comic vocalist," called Little Swills, the Coroner arrives and is conducted into the Sol's Arms by the beadle and the landlord of that place.

The jury is quickly called to order and properly sworn, and the coroner loudly and officiously begins to present to the jury the results of the beadle's investigation. According to a Mrs. Piper, the first witness called, and, "who had a good deal to say … but not much to tell," Nemo was a rather solitary man. She had, however, observed him talking on a number of occasions to Jo, a poor crossing sweeper.

Since Jo is not present in the court when his name is introduced, a hurried search of the neighborhood by the foolish beadle produces him to be questioned. Jo, frightened by the conspicuous nature of the proceedings, soon proves to be an unacceptable witness. He "can't exactly say what'll be done to him after he's dead if he tells a lie to the gentleman here."

As these proceedings progress, they are watched earnestly and with hidden amusement by Mr. Tulkinghorn, present because he was one of the finders of the body. When Jo, the crossing sweep, is rejected by the coroner and the jury retires to consider their verdict, Mr. Tulkinghorn gently questions him.

In this manner, he discovers the deceased Nemo to have been a kindly man who shared what little he had with the poor crossing sweep.

The jury returns quickly and under the prompting of the Coroner agrees to a verdict of accidental death. The jurymen are discharged and the crowd around the courtroom quickly disperses. Little Swills, commended by the landlord of the Sol's Arms, prepares for the evening's entertainment at which he will do his imitation of the Coroner.

Later that night, when all have left, Jo goes to the gate of the poor churchyard where Nemo has been hurriedly buried. Here he holds on to the iron gate looking in a while, and then departs muttering. "He was very good to me, he was!"

Comment

Through the medium of Mr. Tulkinghorn, diverse plot elements are now brought together. The Dedlocks and Lady Dedlock's mysterious interest in the writer of the documents, which had so affected her, have aroused the curiosity of Mr. Tulkinghorn. As a result, he has pursued a new strand possibly connected with the Jarndyce and Jarndyce suit.

CHAPTER TWELVE: ON THE WATCH

At last it has stopped raining in Lincolnshire and Sir Leicester and Lady Dedlock are returning from Paris to Chesney Wold. As they travel in the carriage, Lady Dedlock is happy to have left Paris, for she has been wearied and bored. Sir Leicester is, of course, saved from boredom by contemplation of his own greatness and his morning's correspondence, among which a letter from Mr. Tulkinghorn relates the progress of his suit against Mr. Boythorn. Mr. Tulkinghorn has also included a note to Lady Dedlock, telling her that he has further information concerning the person who copied the affidavit in the Chancery suit. At this news she alights from the carriage to walk for a few minutes.

The Dedlocks are greeted at Chesney Word by Mr. Rouncewell and Rosa, whom Lady Dedlock finds very pretty. Shortly after Lady Dedlock's arrival, the winter social season is in full swing. "All the mirrors in the house are brought into action now," reflecting all sorts of faces, ladies and gentlemen of the newest fashion. They talk incessantly and foolishingly of all sorts of things. Among them are Lord Boodle and William Buffy M.P. who see that the country is going to ruin although they can't quite understand why, or what to do about it. There are others in the gathering "who are agreed to put a smooth glaze on the world, and its realities." In short, they talk of everything, and anything, and nothing.

Among the servants of those empty-headed and foolish people, the same concern with pettiness is repeated. Hortense, Lady Dedlock's personal maid, angered by milady's attention to Rosa, has for several days made fun of Rosa to the other servants.

All of the many rooms of Chesney World are occupied with the exception of the turret chamber, which is always held in readiness for Mr. Tulkinghorn, who might come at any time. Although Lady Dedlock asks for him every night for several days, she is always informed that he has not come. Finally one evening he arrives to tell Sir Leicester and Lady Dedlock what he knows about the writer of the affidavit. He tells of finding Mr. Nemo dead and of the surgeon's suspicion that the man had once known better times. Aside from the fact that the man's name was Nemo, Mr. Tulkinghorn is able to add nothing, since there were no papers or other identification to be found among his effects. As Sir Leicester listens with aversion, Lady Dedlock pretends only a passing interest in the tale, a pretense which does not deceive Mr. Tulkinghorn.

Comment

Among the most detested targets of Dickens' social criticism was the world of fashionable people. Although he rose from "shabby gentility" to rub elbows with the great of the world, Dickens never lost his aversion to those who had inherited great wealth or title and who were content to rest upon these inherited privileges, rather than do something which might make the world a better place.

As a result, it is in these portrayals that Dickens most often is wide of the mark. Rarely does he draw a convincing portrait of the upper classes. He is more at home when he portrays the middle or lower classes.

CHAPTER THIRTEEN: ESTHER'S NARRATIVE

Although Esther, Ada, Richard, and Mr. Jarndyce have held many consultations on the subject of Richard's future, no progress has yet been made in that direction. "He (Richard) had been eight years at a public school, and had learned, I understood, to make Latin verses of several sorts in the most admirable manner. But I never heard that it was anybody's business to find what his natural bent was." Nor has Richard yet discovered his "natural bent." Although he is agreeable to all suggestions, law and medicine among them, the only thing he is sure of is that he doesn't want to go into the Church. Even Mr. Boythorn, who had interested himself in Richard's plight, can offer nothing constructive.

Finally after long discussion, Richard decides one day that being a surgeon is "the very thing." Although Esther suspects that Richard's choice was made merely to solve the continuing dilemma and Mr. Jarndyce cautiously questions him on the subject over a period of time, Richard remains firm in his choice. Required still, however, is the permission of the Chancery Court, of which Richard is still a ward.

Mr. Kenge, Mr. Jarndyce's lawyer, called to represent Richard in this matter before the Chancery, not only agrees that Richard has made an excellent choice of profession, but just happens to have a cousin in the medical profession who might be glad to undertake Richard's education.

It is then quickly settled that a proposed visit to London with Mr. Jarndyce now be combined with Richard's apprenticeship to Mr. Bayham Badger, Mr. Kenge's cousin. Thus, accompanied by Mr. Boythorn, the little group takes up temporary quarters in Oxford Street and makes the rounds of the principal theaters. It seems as if Mr. Guppy is always present in the audience, gazing constantly at Esther, much to her embarrassment. In fact, wherever Esther goes, Mr. Guppy seems to be.

One day when matters are concluded between Mr. Badger and Richard, the little group is invited to dinner at the Badger's home. Here they are greeted by Mrs. Badger, a formidable lady who has had two previous husbands, each greatly admired by the present Mr. Badger. They were a certain captain Swosser, late of the Royal Navy, and a professor Dingo, a man of "European reputation." Everywhere in the Badger household portraits and mementoes of the two previous husbands can be seen.

When they return to their own quarters that evening, Ada reveals to Esther that she and Richard are in love, a fact obvious to all who know them. She then asks that Esther act as intermediary with Mr. Jarndyce. Overjoyed when he hears the news, he urges Richard to work hard at his chosen profession in order to prepare himself for the responsibility of caring for Ada.

These matters concluded, arrangements are made for Richard to leave and assume his studies while Ada remains at Bleak House in the care of Esther.

Comment

Dickens expands his attack on Victorian institutions to include the public schools, which were not really public, but private schools dedicated to the education of the sons of gentlemen. At these schools the curriculum was composed of Latin grammar and composition rather than upon some practical or useful study.

Richard's apprenticeship to Mr. Badger reveals the customary method by which professional men were trained in the nineteenth century. Since there were no formal schools for the study of law or medicine those who wished to follow those professions were apprenticed to practitioners. The great universities of Oxford and Cambridge were at this time actually Divinity Schools where men were trained for the ministry in the Anglican Church.

CHAPTER FOURTEEN: DEPORTMENT

Twice Esther, Ada, and Mr. Jarndyce have missed the Jellybys at home during their London visit, since Mrs. Jellyby seems forever occupied with her philanthropies. Later, however, Caddy Jellyby, accompanied by Peepy, surprises Esther and Ada with a visit during which she reveals to them that she has, since their last meeting, become engaged to a dancing instructor, a Mr. Prince Turveydrop. While Peepy plays beneath a piano, Caddy relates the difficulties of the Jellyby household. Mrs. Jellyby's philanthropies have brought Mr. Jellyby to near financial ruin and Mrs. Jellyby still expects Caddy to marry Mr. Quale.

Since Caddy seems so much improved in spirit and appearance, Esther is anxious to help her. She arranges to go with Caddy and Peepy to Mr. Turveydrop's Academy to meet the fiance, and later with Caddy to meet Ada and Mr. Jarndyce at Miss Flite's. At the Academy she meets Prince, the fiance, an amiable young man who works twelve hours a day to support his father, a fat, fashionable old man who "fully believed himself to be one of the aristocracy."

Later, as they walk to Miss Flite's, Esther, touched by Caddy's plight, promises to become her friend and to help Caddy to improve herself. When they arrive at Krook's bottle shop they find the door open. Going in they find Ada and Mr. Jarndyce talking to a Mr. Woodcourt, a young physician attending to Miss Flite since Miss Flite "alarmed at the occurrence in the house" (the death of Mr. Nemo), had fallen ill and was being treated by the kindly Mr. Woodcourt.

As the group talks, they are interrupted by a visit from Krook, who is much interested in the case of Jarndyce and Jarndyce. He displays an intense interest in Mr. Jarndyce whom he detains "under one pretense or another" while the group inspects the Chancery (the Bottle Shop). The tour finished at last, Krook reveals to Mr. Jarndyce his desire to learn to read, although he would not trust anyone to teach him for fear "they might teach (him) wrong."

The strange conversation of Krook causes Mr. Jarndyce to inquire of Mr. Woodcourt if Krook is mentally deranged. To this question the young surgeon replies "No." Finally as they leave, Mr. Jarndyce invites Mr. Woodcourt, whom they had previously met at Mr. Badger's, to dinner that day.

Comment

Although in the person of old Mr. Turveydrop, Dickens makes fun of dandyism, he was something of the dandy himself - both careful and dramatic in his dress.

CHAPTER FIFTEEN: BELL YARD

While in London, Mr. Jarndyce is constantly beset by crowds of excitable philanthropists, including Mr. Quale, Mrs. Pardiggle, and Mr. Gusher, each of whom seems so eloquent on behalf of the others that the "wind was east for three whole weeks." (Mr. Jarndyce is disturbed.) As usual, this noisy and ineffectual group, anxious to help the poor and downtrodden, and incidentally themselves, had gathered around a likely source of revenue in the kindly Mr. Jarndyce.

Fortunately for Mr. Jarndyce, relief was forthcoming in the person of Mr. Harold Skimpole, who is, as usual, in difficulty because he has failed to pay a bill. This time his butcher has instituted legal proceedings, and even now the bailiff occupies his house - not, however, the previous bailiff, Coavinses, but a new bailiff. As Skimpole informs Mr. Jarndyce and Esther, "Coavinses has been arrested by the great bailiff" (has died) and has left three children, who, being motherless, are now at a great "disadvantage" since Coavinses, profession was "unpopular."

Disturbed by the news, Mr. Jarndyce, Esther, and Ada, accompanied by Skimpole, go to Coavinses' "castle," where they discover two small children, Tom and Emma, locked in a room. They had been locked in by "Charley" (Charlotte, an older sister of thirteen) who left the key in the keeping of Mrs. Binder, the landlady. When Mrs. Binder opens the room, they discover Tom (five), carefully nursing Emma eighteen months), while "Charley" went about the neighborhood trying to support them by washing clothes. Although Mrs. Binder has herself been kind (by remitting the rent), as have some other neighbors, the children's lot is still difficult because their father had been unpopular with the neighbors.

As Mr. Jarndyce and Mrs. Binder talk, they are interrupted by Mr. Gridley, a downstairs boarder, a stern and gruff man, who along with Mrs. Binder had been helping "Charley" to care for Tom and Emma. Further talk with the "irascible" and impolite Gridley, reveals him to be "the man from Shropshire" (Chapter One) whose case has been so long in Chancery.

When Mr. Gridley learns Mr. Jarndyce's name, he recognizes him as a kindred soul, and relates the story of his own difficulties with the Court of Chancery. He and his brother, involved in a dispute over a small legacy, have become so enmeshed in the proceedings of the court that they have already spent more than three times the total amount of the legacy without any hope of a solution. Now almost destroyed as a man, he returns almost daily to the Court of Chancery. As he explains it, "I'll shame them…. If I knew I was going to die and could be carried there, and had a voice to speak with, I would die there saying, "You have brought me here, and sent me from here many a time. Now send me out feet foremost.'"

Comment

Through the character of Gridley, Dickens becomes more violent in his attack upon Chancery. Coavinses is sometimes called Neckett.

BLEAK HOUSE

. . . .

CHAPTER SIXTEEN: TOM-ALL-ALONE'S

As Sir Leicester Dedlock awaits at Chesney Wold, nursing his share of the family gout, Lady Dedlock goes to London. There, disguised as a servant, she goes to Tom-All-Alone's, a dirty, ruined street filled with helpless humanity and decayed buildings, a street whose buildings are part of the famous Jarndyce and Jarndyce estate. Here, deceiving no one, for her manners reveal her as a gentlewoman, she seeks out Jo, the crossing sweeper, whose name she had read in the newspapers as a witness in the inquest into the death of Nemo.

Offered money by the disguised Lady Dedlock, Jo takes her to the grave of the unfortunate Nemo. On the way, he points out to her Krook's Bottle Shop where Nemo had lived, and takes her past Snagsby's stationery where he had been employed. At the grave, she stares horrified, looking at the spot barely covered by a pile of bones where Mr. Nemo lies. She asks Jo to point out the spot again, and as he does so she slips away. Jo, finding himself alone, returns to Tom-All-Alone's, examining by gaslight the gold piece which Lady Dedlock has given him.

Comment

Again Dickens takes time to draw various plot elements together. Lady Dedlock's interest in Nemo is revealed as more than casual. At the chapter's close, the ghost is heard to walk more distinctly than ever at Chesney Wold, **foreshadowing** some evil tidings for that house.

CHAPTER SEVENTEEN: ESTHER'S NARRATIVE

Because the schools in which Richard has been educated as a youngster have failed to instill in him the need for concentration or application to any study, he soon discovers that he is not really interested in medicine. This fact, first revealed to Esther by Mrs. Bayham Badger, is later admitted by Richard, who speculates, "If I went into Mr. Kenge's office... I should be able to look after Ada's interest and my own interests." Although he is disappointed, Mr. Jarndyce receives the news without anger and cautions Richard against impatience in seeking a new field of study.

Late one evening, as she is about to retire, Esther is detained by Mr. Jarndyce, who feels that now, since she is twenty-one, she ought to know what little he can tell her of her past. He tells her that, nine years before, he received a letter from Miss Barbary (Esther's aunt) asking his help for Esther in the event of Miss Barbary's death. Agreeing to this request, Mr. Jarndyce made arrangements through Mr. Kenge (his lawyer) without ever seeing Miss Barbary.

The next morning, Mr. Woodcourt, accompanied by his mother, comes to bid them all goodbye, since he is leaving for China and India as a ship's surgeon because he needs the money to continue in his profession. His mother, an impoverished but proud woman, who traces her ancestry to Welsh royalty, suggests to her son that, wherever he goes he should, "remember his pedigree, and ... on no account form an alliance below it," a suggestion which unaccountably distresses Mr. Woodcourt and pains Esther. Shortly after they leave, Caddy Jellyby arrives bearing a bouquet of flowers, which she explains had been left at Miss Flite's for Esther by somebody who "was hurrying away an hour ago to join a ship."

Comment

Richard's failure at medicine is a **foreshadowing** of other failures to come, and a continuing indictment of the Court of Chancery and the schools which were largely responsible for his failure.

CHAPTER EIGHTEEN: LADY DEDLOCK

After much indecision, Richard finally decides to try law and enters "on an experimental course of Messrs. Kenge and Carboy." This matter settled for the moment, Esther, Ada, and Mr. Jarndyce, accompanied by Harold Skimpole, leave London for a visit to Mr. Bovthorn's place in Lincolnshire. On the way, they are met by Mr. Boythorn with an open carriage, and are forced to drive around Chesney Wold, since the feud between Sir Leicester Dedlock and Mr. Boythorn still continues.

On Sunday morning all attend service at a little church in the park, which is also attended by the Dedlocks. Here Esther becomes aware of a strange attraction, a familiarity, with Lady Dedlock although she has never before seen her. Mr. Skimpole is, of course, much taken with Sir Leicester Dedlock, whom he sees as a potential patron, much to the consternation of Mr. Boythorn who thinks Mr. Skimpole unprincipled. Mr. Jarndyce, who still pays Mr. Skimpole's bills, simply laughs at the "childlike" Mr. Skimpole's seemingly unconscious dishonesty.

While wandering through Chesney Wold's park one afternoon, Esther, Ada, and Mr. Jarndyce are caught in a rainstorm and take refuge in a lodge. Here they are soon joined by Lady Dedlock, who has been caught in the same storm. As Mr. Jarndyce and Lady Dedlock talk, Esther becomes aware that Mr. Jarndyce has known Lady Dedlock, and a sister from whom she had been separated, for some time. (Although this is not yet revealed, Lady Dedlock's sister was Miss Barbary, Esther's aunt.)

When a carriage arrives for Lady Dedlock, both Rosa and Hortense alight, each feeling she had been sent for. As Lady Dedlock drives off with Rosa, leaving Hortense behind, violent hatred is visible on Hortense's face.

Comment

Two new developments are revealed in this chapter. First, that there is a mysterious relationship between Esther and Lady Dedlock, of which Esther is vaguely aware. Second, the reader's opinion of Harold Skimpole is altered. We begin to see him more as an opportunist, as does Mr. Boythorn, rather than the "childlike" innocent Mr. Jarndyce sees.

CHAPTER NINETEEN: MOVING ON

The Court of Chancery is closed during the summer when most people have left London. Among those who remain are Mr. and Mrs. Snagsby, who are expecting Mr. and Mrs. Chadband to dinner. Mr. Chadband is a self-styled preacher, a fat, oily man who preaches loudly and constantly to all who will listen. As they eat, they are interrupted by the arrival of a policeman who has arrested Jo for loitering and for refusing his command to "move on." Poor Jo simply does not know how to respond to this often repeated command, for there is nowhere for him "to move on" to. Finally, Jo is left for the moment with Mr. Snagsby, who will see that he does "move on."

This matter for the moment settled, Mr. Guppy, at whose suggestion the policeman brought Jo to Mr. Snagsby's, questions Jo about the mysterious lady who had given him the money found in his possession. He then turns his attention to Mrs. Chadband and subjects her to his legal cross-examination and discovers that she had once been "left in charge of a child named Esther Summerson."

As this exchange between Mrs. Chadband and Mr. Guppy continues, Mr. Chadband sermonizes to poor Jo, who finally manages to escape. He goes then to Blackfriars' Bridge and there eats the food which Mr. Snagsby has given him while he looks "up at the great cross on St. Paul's Cathedral. Here he remains watching the crowd until he is told "to move on."

Comment

Through repetition of the meaningless command "to move on," Dickens satirizes England's attempts at a solution to the problems of poverty. He particularly satirizes the optimistic belief of many parliamentarians that great progress was being made.

CHAPTER TWENTY: A NEW LODGER

At the office of Kenge and Carboy only Guppy, Richard, and a young boy called Smallweed remain, for everyone else is out of town. Here Mr. Guppy, suspicious of Richard, whom he regards as a "swell," is admired by the fifteen-year-old Smallweed, who aspires to be like him and is visited by Tony Jobling, an unemployed friend, whom Guppy takes to dinner. After feeding the starved Jobling, Guppy proposes that Jobling take up residence at Krook's, under the name of Mr. Weevle, and there discover what he can of interest. In turn, Guppy promises to supply Jobling's needs as well as secure a job for him as law-writer for Mr. Snagsby.

Arrangements are quickly made and the next day Mr. Krook happily accepts Mr. Weevle as his boarder. Here Jobling (as Weevle) quickly establishes himself on familiar terms with Krook and the neighbors. In his free time he avidly reads the newspapers for any scrap of society news which might be of some later use.

Comment

Jobling's name describes his person. He is a Job-ling, a person available for small "jobs."

CHAPTER TWENTY-ONE: THE SMALLWEED FAMILY

The Smallweed family is composed of Bartholomew, Guppy's admirer and co-worker; Grandfather Smallweed, a paralyzed moneylender who lends money at usurious rates; Grandmother Smallweed, a feeble-minded old woman who bears the brunt of her husband's temper; Judy Smallweed, Bart's twin sister (who in character closely resembles her grandfather); and "Charley" (Charlotte, Coavinses' daughter), the family servant who suffers from the family's inhumane treatment.

Among the visitors to the Smallweed house is a Mr. George, who appears to have once been a trooper (soldier). He is a good-looking man of fifty who has gotten involved with the Smallweeds by having answered a newspaper advertisement about a Captain Hawdon, a missing army friend supposed to have been lost at sea. Although he is in financial difficulty, because of his efforts to make payments on the principal and interest of the debt to Grandfather Smallweed, he refuses to seek co-signers so that he may receive additional loans.

Afterward Mr. George returns to his shooting gallery, where he is greeted by Phil Squod, a grotesque but powerful little man who acts as his assistant. Like Mr. George, he is a man who has no natural home, having always been a vagabond. Thus, between the two, there springs a common bond which cements their friendship.

Comment

Mr. George is Mrs. Rouncewell's son George who had many years before run away and joined the army and from whom she had never heard.

Grandfather Smallweed and Phil Squod help to fill Dickens' famous gallery of grotesque characters, although they are persons of vastly different temperament.

CHAPTER TWENTY-TWO: MR. BUCKET

Mr. Tulkinghorn and Mr. Bucket, a "sharp-eyed" detective he has hired to help discover the identity of the servant woman who had gone to Mr. Nemo's grave with Jo, secure Mr. Snagsby's help in finding Jo. Convinced that they mean Jo no harm and sworn to secrecy, Snagsby leads them to Tom-All-Alone's street, "a villainous street, undrained, unventilated, deep in black mud and corrupt water," and there in a dilapidated house they meet the two brickmakers from St. Albans and their wives, Jenny and Liz. As they talk to Jenny, who is nursing the child of her friend, she pathetically recalls her own child who had died. Finally, Jo returns carrying a bottle of medicine for which he had been sent.

Bucket, Mr. Tulkinghorn, Mr. Snagsby and Jo, return to Tulkinghorn's house where they confront Jo with a veiled lady whom Jo identifies as "the lady. When she is revealed as Hortense, Lady Dedlock's ex-maid, Jo realizes that she is not the same woman because her hands and voice were different, although her veil and bonnet were identical with the mysterious lady's.

Mr. Tulkinghorn has thus achieved the object of his search. He is certain that Lady Dedlock is the woman whom Jo led to Nemo's grave, although he is still uncertain as to why she went there.

Comment

Again Dickens uses the melodramatic device of coincidence. These are the same brickmakers and family we met in Chapter Eight.

CHAPTER TWENTY-THREE: ESTHER'S NARRATIVE

Returning to Bleak House, after six weeks, at Mr. Boythorn's, Esther is surprised by a visit from Hortense, Lady Dedlock's former maid, who is seeking employment. Assuring Hortense that she has no need of an attendant, Esther is glad to bring the conference to a close.

At Bleak House, Esther, Ada, and Mr. Jarndyce are visited every Saturday and Sunday by Richard, who claims he has "got at the core of the mystery" (the Jarndyce case), and that, like Miss Flite, he has begun to haunt the Court (Chancery). He also reveals to Esther that he means to give up the study of law, since he believes that he has solved the Jarndyce suit. He has now resolved to go into the army as a means of relieving the debts which he has recently amassed. As Esther listens, her heart aches, for she wonders how this will end. Earnestly she implores Richard, "not to put any trust in Chancery."

Later, meeting Caddy Jellyby and her fiance, Prince, Esther advises them to reveal their engagement to their respective parents. With Esther, they go first to Mr. Turveydrop, who, although at first disturbed by the news, eagerly assents when assured that the young couple will make him "our first consideration." Later, Mrs. Jellyby, more annoyed at the interruption of her "African affairs" than anything else, also gives her reluctant consent.

Happy that these matters were now concluded, Esther arrives home where she finds "a present ... with Mr. Jarndyce's love," waiting for her. It was "Charley" (Charlotte), whom Mr. Jarndyce has hired as a maid for Esther. Charley quickly informs her that Tom is now at school and that Emma has been left with Mrs. Blinder and is "being took such care of." At this kindness, Esther breaks into tears of joy in which she is soon joined by Charley.

Comment

Again Dickens pauses to tie together diverse plot elements. Richard's new career is introduced, Caddy Jellyby's engagement is settled, and arrangements are completed for the care of the Neckett family.

CHAPTER TWENTY-FOUR: AN APPEAL CASE

Following Richard's account to Esther of his change of heart regarding the Law, Mr. Jarndyce is advised, and arrangements are made through Chancery (for Richard is still a ward), for him to enter the army. His name is entered as an applicant for an ensign's commission in the Horse Guards and the purchase money is deposited with an agent. However, Mr. Jarndyce, seriously disturbed by Richard's instability, suggests that Richard and Ada break their engagement until such time as Richard is more firmly established. Although Ada quietly accepts her guardian's suggestion, Richard feels greatly hurt by it.

He then violently throws himself into preparation for his new career. While at Bleak House, he gets "up at five o'clock every morning to practice the broad-sword exercise," and in

London he arranges for fencing lessons with an ex-cavalryman (George Rouncewell), who, when introduced to Esther feels strongly that he has met her before. George's discovery that Mr. Jarndyce is party to a Chancery suit, cause him to comment on another such suitor who worked off his frustrations at George's shooting gallery. That suitor, revealed as Mr. Gridly, the man from Shropshire, is at that moment in hiding at George's galley since he is being sought, under a peace warrant, for arguing with the magistrate at the Chancery.

On the morning of the day appointed for Richard's departure, the case of Jarndyce and Jarndyce is again scheduled to be presented in Chancery, this time" for further directions, about some bill of costs." There Esther, Ada, Richard, and Mr. Jarndyce are greeted by Mr. Kenge and joined by the ever-present Miss Elite while they watch the ponderous operation of that involved institution. As usual, the proceedings are brief, and the case is, as usual, "referred back for the present."

As they leave the court, they are accosted by Mr. Guppy, present in his official capacity for Kenge and Carboy, who desires to introduce Esther to Mrs. Chadband, who turns out to be Mrs. Rachael, her godmother's former housekeeper. Chilled by the unexpected encounter, Esther, along with Richard, is then unexpectedly met by Mr. George, who explains that he is seeking Miss Elite.

George then explains that Mr. Gridly, hiding at his gallery, is dying and wishes to see Miss Elite, since they had shared so many trials together. Accompanied by Ada and Richard, Esther and George quickly go to the gallery, where they discover and old gentleman who tells them he is a physician come to see a sick man. Once inside, however, he reveals himself as Inspector

Bucket and states that he has come to arrest Mr. Gridly. However, with the discovery that Mr. Gridly is dying, Inspector Bucket kindly attempts to encourage him to live, but to no avail. The exhausted and worn out Mr. Gridly dies, finally escaping the toils of the system which had so long enmeshed him.

Comment

George seems to recognize Esther because of the great resemblance she bears to Lady Dedlock, later to be revealed as her mother.

The purchase of a commission for Richard reveals the usual method by which commissions were dispensed in the British Army during the Victorian period.

CHAPTER TWENTY-FIVE: MRS. SNAGSBY SEES IT ALL

Mr. Snagsby, disturbed by his involvement with Mr. Bucket and Mr. Tulkinghorn, has undergone a change which is noted by his wife. Determined to discover the causes of his change, she observes "various signs and tokens" (his mail, his pockets, his conversations), and concludes that Jo is Mr. Snagsby's son - the result of some concealed relationship in the past. Arranging for Jo to be present at the Snagsby home in Cook's Court, she has the oily Reverend Chadband preach one of his wordy sermons on the subject of sin and unnatural parents, while she observes further the actions of Mr. Snagsby and Jo. Finally, as Jo sits uncomprehending and poor Mr. Snagsby hides behind the parlor door, Mrs. Snagsby, goaded by her suspicions, goes into a violent fit.

Wandering into the kitchen, Jo is met by Guster, who, discovering that he is also an orphan, shares her supper with him. As Jo leaves, Mr. Snagsby gives him a half crown and admonishes him to remain silent about the mysterious lady. Unfortunately, they are observed by the watchful Mrs. Snagsby, who feels all her suspicions now confirmed.

Comment

Some comic relief is supplied, in an otherwise serious novel, by Mrs. Snagsby's ridiculous suspicion of her meek husband.

CHAPTER TWENTY-SIX: SHARPSHOOTERS

As George and his assistant Phil discuss Phil's early years as a tinker and the accident which had crippled him, they are disturbed by a visit from Mr. Smallweed and Mrs. Smallweed. The Smallweeds wish a "fragment of Captain Hawdon's writing" for a lawyer (Mr. Tulkinghorn) since those samples in his possession are inadequate. George, suspicious of the old usurer, refuses and Mr. Smallweed is forced to persuade George to go with him to Mr. Tulkinghorn's so that Tulkinghorn may explain the purpose for his request in person.

Comment

Mr. Tulkinghorn needs a larger sample of handwriting to confirm his suspicion that Captain Hawdon was really Mr. Nemo, in order to further establish Lady Dedlock's relationship with that mysterious individual.

CHAPTER TWENTY-SEVEN: MORE OLD SOLDIERS
THAN ONE

After Mr. Smallweed, Judy, and George arrived at Mr. Tulkinghorn's, Mr. Tulkinghorn produces for George samples of Nemo's handwriting (affidavits) and attempts to secure the information from George as to whether or not they are samples of Captain Hawdon's handwriting. However, George, still suspicious since Mr. Tulkinghorn refuses to reveal his reason for wanting either the sample of handwriting or information about the handwriting in the affidavits, steadfastly refuses to give any information. Although offered money by Mr. Tulkinghorn, George, "feeling smothered at present" by these pressures, insists that he first consult an old soldier friend who is more an authority in these matters, and immediately leaves for that consultation. Remaining behind with Mr. Tulkinghorn, who keeps calm, Mr. Smallweed is angered by George's refusal and promises Mr. Tulkinghorn that he will bring to bear whatever pressure he can (George is in debt to him) to make George reveal whatever Mr. Tulkinghorn requires.

At the home of his old friend Matthew Bagnet, a former artilleryman who now conducts a musician's shop on the southern edge of London, George is greeted by Mrs. Bagnet, a bluff, hearty woman and two of her children, Quebec and Malta, so named "from the places of their birth in barracks."

They are soon found by Matthew and Woolrich (the only Bagnet child born in Britain) who had been playing a theater engagement. After dinner George is advised by Matthew (actually through Mrs. Bagnet without whose advice Matthew does or says nothing) to tell Mr. Tulkinghorn nothing unless he is more open than at present. Although Matthew is lavish in praise of his wife, and is a willing recipient of her advice, he tells

George that he "never owns to it before her." Although "the old girl" is a treasure, "discipline must be maintained."

Returning to Tulkinghorn's, George advises that angry gentleman of his decision to remain silent and then returns to his shooting gallery.

Comment

Through a common connection with the Smallweeds, various plot elements are again brought together.

CHAPTER TWENTY-EIGHT: THE IRONMASTER

At the moment Chesney Wold is filled with poor relations, nobodies, all claiming to be cousins, more or less, of some remote degree. Of these, foremost stands Volumnia Dedlock, "long considered a bore to mankind" who lives at Bath on an annual pension from Sir Leicester, and who makes "occasional resurrections at the country houses of her cousins." All these cousins, along with William Buffy, who found, when he tried to secure a pension for Volumnia, that "these were not the times when it could be done." The honorable Bob Staple, who, although he could shoot like a gamekeeper, could not acquire a well-paying post in the service of his country, which required no trouble or responsibility, agreed heartily with Sir Leicester's opinion that "the country was going to pieces." Indeed, this opinion is confirmed by news that Mrs. Rouncewell's son (the Ironmaster) is going to run for Parliament.

When Mr. Rouncewell arrives later to ask Sir Leicester's release of Rosa so that she can marry his son Watt, and explains that he first wishes Rosa to be properly educated for that occasion, Sir Leicester is annoyed. Feeling that the need for such further education is a reflection on the village school, which he supports, and that Mr. Rouncewell a man "getting out of his station." As a result Sir Leicester politely but haughtily announces that Rosa is free to do as she chooses, and, as Mr. Rouncewell leaves, he announces his intention of discouraging his son's attentions to Rosa.

Later, Lady Dedlock questions Rosa on her relationship with Watt, and promises to make her happy, "If I can make anybody happy on earth." After Rosa withdraws, she stares at the fire and listens to sounds from the Ghost's Walk.

Comment

Again Dickens levels his attack upon the aristocracy whom he contrasts with the new generations of producers, with men of accomplishment rather than of birth. Like a **refrain**, the sound of the ghost's footsteps outside Chesney Wold foretells of disgrace soon to overtake that house.

CHAPTER TWENTY-NINE: THE YOUNG MAN

With Chesney Wold closed for the season, the Dedlocks are in London. Here Sir Leicester sits before the fire reading a newspaper in his library. Finding an article about the present degraded state of society, he goes to Lady Dedlock's room where he proceeds to read to her, offering grave comments about the very truth of the articles while she listens, bored. They are interrupted by Guppy, who has come to see Lady Dedlock. Although annoyed by the intrusion, Sir Leicester retires and

Guppy, who has written Lady Dedlock many letters, reveals the nature of his visit.

After receiving assurance that Lady Dedlock will not report his visit to Kenge and Carboy, he reveals that he is in love with Esther Summerson and has been trying to clear up the mystery of her past, so that he might find favor in his eyes. As a result of his researches, he has made numerous discoveries. Among them he has noted the resemblance between Esther and Lady Dedlock, a discovery first inspired by Lady Dedlock's picture at Chesney Wold. In addition, through "professional circumstances," he had met Mrs. Chadband uMrs. Rachael) from whom he had learned that Esther's real name was Hawdon and not Summerson. Finally, to the trembling Lady Dedlock, he relates that there exists evidence that the dead Nemo's real name was actually Captain Hawdon and that he will shortly have in his possession letters, which will reveal Lady Dedlock's intimate acquaintance with both Captain Hawdon and Miss Barbary.

Shaken by these revelations, Lady Dedlock offers Guppy jewelry as the price of the incriminating letters, but he refuses, telling her that he could not accept anything for his services because he is "not actuated by any motives of that sort."

Alone, Lady Dedlock weeps, aware for the first time that her child by Captain Hawdon had not died as she had been told by Miss Barbary, the stern sister who had renounced both Lady Dedlock and the family name.

Comment

Although Esther's past has been hinted at in preceding chapters, the reader learns the truth for the first time with certainty.

BLEAK HOUSE

. . . .

CHAPTER THIRTY: ESTHER'S NARRATIVE

Sometime after Richard's departure for the Army, Bleak House is visited by Mrs. Woodcourt, who, although she intended to stay only a few days, remains "almost three weeks." She talks kindly and confidentially to Esther of her son's royal ancestry (Ap Kerrig, a Welsh king), and of her continuing hopes that he will marry well. Esther enjoys these false conversations and is unaccountably "anxious" that the old lady would like her.

When Caddy Jellyby comes down after Mrs. Woodcourt had left, she brings the news that she is to be married in a month and that Esther and Ada are to be her bridesmaids. Then, after helping Caddy to prepare for the wedding and also to learn housekeeping, Esther returns with her to London, where Mrs. Jellyby, assisted by an "unwholesome boy" dictates letters and "holding Borrioboolan interviews," sits surrounded by wastepaper and letters. As usual, the poor, groaning Mr. Jellyby fends for himself as best he can.

Annoyed at the interruption, and the expense (which might have gone for African affairs), Mrs. Jellyby reluctantly consents to the wedding. Esther and Caddy, assisted by Mr. Jellyby, clean the impossibly dirty room to be used. Finally, as the monumental task nears completion, Mr. Jellyby speaks at greater length to Caddy than he ever has before. If she is to be happy he advises, "Never have a mission."

Among the wedding guests are Mr. and Mrs. Pardiggle, Mr. Quale, and Miss Wisk (philanthropic friends of Mrs. Jellyby), old Mr. Turveydrop, who considers himself "vastly superior to all the company," and Mr. Jarndyce, who "turned it all into an occasion of merry encouragement for Caddy." Finally as the bride and groom are about to leave, Mr. Turveydrop lets it be known that he expects them home in a week. After they leave, Mr. Jellyby, as usual, unable to speak, presses Esther's hands as if to express his gratitude for her help.

Comment

In addition to advancing the plot through Esther's solving of Caddy Jellyby's problems, Dickens repeats his criticisms of misguided philanthropy.

CHAPTER THIRTY-ONE: NURSE AND PATIENT

Shortly after Esther returns to Bleak House, following Caddy's wedding, she is informed by Charley that Jenny and Liz (the brickmakers wives) now in London are nursing a "poor boy." Led by Charley, she then goes to Jenny's, where she discovers Jenny caring for the sick boy (Jo) and for her friend's child, while Liz is out unsuccessfully seeking help. As the veiled Esther enters the room, the nearly delirious Jo, mistaking her for the disguised Lady Dedlock, cries out for fear that she has come to take him "to the berrin ground [cemetery]."

Jo, however, is quickly calmed by the solicitous Jenny, who tells Esther that she found him nearly frozen in Tom-All-Alone's Street early that morning. They are interrupted by the returning Liz, who explains that although she has gone from one official to another seeking help, they have all demonstrated "skill in evading their duties, instead of performing them." Thus with no help forthcoming, and with the intoxicated bricklayers expected home soon, Jenny and Liz give Jo a few half pence, and he leaves for the warmth of a nearby brick kiln.

Esther and "Charley" hurry after the unfortunate Jo and bring him to Bleak House, where he is welcomed by the kindly Mr. Jarndyce, in spite of Harold Skimpole's suggestion to "turn him out." Here, Mr. Jarndyce with an expression "of amusement and indignation" at the "childlike" Skimpole's recommendation, remarks vehemently on a social system which permits the poor to starve while providing the best of care for convicted prisoners.

The next morning they discover that Jo has disappeared and that Charley has fallen ill. Esther nurses the seriously ill Charley from near death, in the isolation of her own room, until, at last, she falls ill herself.

Comment

Again coincidence serves to advance the plot. The reappearance of the brickmakers' wives serves to unite Esther's narrative with that of the deceased Captain Nemo through the medium of Jo, and ultimately leads to Lady Dedlock.

CHAPTER THIRTY-TWO: THE APPOINTED TIME

It is a "close, damp night" in Lincoln's Inn (In the Chancery district) and, as the inhabitants go about their customary pursuits, Mr. Snagsby, "ill at ease" and "impelled by the mystery of which he is partaker," takes a walk in Chancery Lane. Here he meets Mr. Weevle (Jobling) to whom he remarks that the atmosphere this evening is peculiarly "greasy." To this comment, Weevle, who is awaiting the arrival of Mr. Guppy, remarks that "it gives me the horrors." Then passing a few comments on coincidence that both occupants of Mr. Krook's room (Mr. Nemo and Weevle) should have been law writers, Mr. Snagsby departs followed closely by Mrs. Snagsby, who wears a pocket handkerchief over her head.

A little later, Guppy and Weevle are discussing Weevle's progress in securing a packet of letters addressed with the name Hawdon that Krook had earlier shown to Weevle. As they await the time appointed for Weevle to meet Krook, they are aware of the uncomfortable nature of the room. It seems filled with a "thick yellow liquid" which "drips and creeps" over a corner of the room. Finally, at the appointed time, the fearful Weevle goes to meet Krook. Failing to find him, he returns for Mr. Guppy, and together they search the shop. Led by Krook's cat, they find a pile of ashes and a burned patch on the floor in front of the fireplace. In horror, they run for help. Mr. Krook "has died the death of all Lord Chancellors in all events and all places ...." His death is the result of the "spontaneous combustion" of the corrupted humors of the vicious body itself.

Comment

This is among the most famous chapters in all Dickens' work. The oily Mr. Krook's death which Dickens accounts for by spontaneous combustion has been the subject of much critical discussion. In fact, he found it necessary to defend the idea in an introduction attached to all later editions of Bleak House.

CHAPTER THIRTY-THREE: INTERLOPERS

Guppy and Weevle, celebrities now since their discovery of Krook's remains, regale visitors to the Sol's Arms (the tavern where Nemo's inquest was held) with the details of their discovery. The proprietor, Mr. James Bogsby, is overjoyed at the increased business which the strange events in the neighborhood have brought to his tavern. As Guppy and Weevle eat and drink, other denizens of the neighborhood recall having noted a strange odor emanating from Krook's shop on the previous evening. Finally, Guppy and the frightened Weevle, aware that an inquest will be held, prepare a written statement in which they agree to suppress certain aspects of their presence in Mr. Krook's shop on the occasion of the fateful discovery. Although Weevle agrees to this expedient, he tells Guppy that his part in the conspiracy is finished and refuses to return to live over the bottle shop.

Among those who arrive at the Sol's Arms Inn, are the Smallweeds, including Mrs. Smallweed, Judy, Bartholomew, and Grandfather Smallweed, who reveals that since Mr. Krook was Mrs. Smallweed's brother, they have made arrangements through their solicitor, Mr. Tulkinghorn, "to look after the property." A clerk of Mr. Tulkinghorn makes the necessary arrangements with the police, and Mr. Smallweed is carried "on a visit of sentiment" into Krook's shop.

Confusion tends to build at the Sol's Arms with the arrival of numerous "doctors" and "philosophers" who talk learnedly about "inflammable gases," and engage in endless dispute. They are interrupted by the arrival of the Coroner, who, as usual, only adds to the confusion.

Guppy, realizing that he cannot now secure the letters that he has promised to Lady Dedlock, leaves to tell her so. Here he is recognized by Mr. Tulkinghorn who is suspicious of his (Guppy's) visit to Lady Dedlock.

Comment

Some plot elements are now joined. A connection is established between the Smallweeds and Mr. Krook, and Mr. Tulkinghorn becomes aware of Mr. Guppy's involvement with Lady Dedlock.

CHAPTER THIRTY-FOUR: A TURN OF THE SCREW

Opening a letter, George Rouncewell finds Mr. Smallweed's demand for immediate payment of a debt which he has previously renewed at usurious rates of interest. George immediately goes to see Matthew Bagnet, who had co-signed the note and will now have to pay it. Rebuking George, through his "old girl" (Mrs. Bagnet), "forever taking this business (the Shooting Gallery) without the means," Matthew, and George, go to see Mr. Smallweed. When Smallweed finds they do not have the money he sends them angrily to see his lawyer.

At Mr. Tulkinghorn's, they are kept waiting more than an hour. Later, George, in private, offers Mr. Tulkinghorn the letters of Captain Hawdon, which Tulkinghorn had previously sought, in exchange for Mr. Bagnet's release from the consequences of the debt. Mr. Tulkinghorn accepts the offer and the debt is restored to its original basis without the involvement of Matthew Bagnet.

Comment

Although Mrs. Rouncewell almost meets her son George as she emerges from Mr. Tulkinghorn's office, they fail to recognize each other.

CHAPTER THIRTY-FIVE: ESTHER'S NARRATIVE

Still very weak and changed by her illness, Esther finally permits Mr. Jarndyce to visit her. As he tells her of the concern which her illness has aroused in Ada and him, he is forced to tell Esther of the growing gulf between himself and Richard, who now suspects him of having "conflicting interests" in the Jarndyce and Jarndyce case. Both Esther and Mr. Jarndyce, deeply disturbed by this, wish that poor Richard, who has been so altered by that fateful case, could be "restored to his proper nature."

Arrangements are made for a visit from Miss Flite, who once "walked twenty-miles" to Bleak House when she had heard of Esther's illness. Arriving on the appointed day, Miss Flite relates the strange story of a lady who bought a handkerchief of Esther's from Jenny, the brickmaker's wife. Esther, thinking the lady perhaps Caddy, does not give the matter much thought as Miss Flite recounts of her own experiences in Chancery and warns that someone must hold Richard back from the same sort of fate, "or he'll be drawn to ruin."

Miss Flite also surprises Esther with the information that Mr. Woodcourt has been the hero of a shipwreck in the East

Indian Sea. Esther is relieved, since she is so changed by her illness that Mr. Woodcourt has not spoken to her of the love which she feels certain he holds for her.

Comment

In Mr. Jarndyce's comments on the changes in Richard, Dickens reinforces his criticism against the Court of Chancery through cause and effect; i.e., the effect produced in Richard is caused by his lifetime involvement in the Chancery suit.

CHAPTER THIRTY-SIX: CHESNEY WOLD

Accompanied by Charley and Mr. Jarndyce, Esther journeys to Mr. Boythorn's in Lincolnshire to recuperate from her illness. Here, for the first time since her illness, she looks in the glass and realizing that she was much altered, makes plans with Charley for her recovery in the fresh air of Lincolnshire.

A favorite outdoor spot of Esther's is park woods of Chesney Wold (next door to Mr. Boythorn's) where there is a fine view of the famous Ghost's Walk. She is startled here one day by the approach of Lady Dedlock, who carries in her hand the handkerchief with which Esther had earlier covered Jenny's dead baby. In a burst of emotion, Lady Dedlock reveals to Esther that she is her "wicked and unhappy mother." As Esther embraces her, the tearful Lady Dedlock asks that what she has revealed be kept secret, for the sake of Sir Leicester and herself, although she allows Esther to "confide fully" in Mr. Jarndyce. Before she departs she gives Esther a letter containing the secrets of her birth, and tells Esther of her fear that the secret may soon be discovered by Mr. Tulkinghorn.

Later, alone in her room, Esther reads the letter, which tells how Esther's aunt (Miss Barbary) had concealed from Lady Dedlock the fact that her child had lived, and had "with no desire or willingness, reared (her) in strictest secrecy." After carefully burning the letter, Esther cries herself to sleep, recalling the fearful woman who raised her and feeling that she should have died at birth.

The next day, as Esther walks alone near Chesney Wold, she finds herself on Ghost's Walk. Suddenly, listening to the echo of her own footsteps and recalling the dreadful legend of the walk, she becomes aware that it is she who is to bring calamity upon the stately house, and she flees in terror to her room. Here, after reading loving letters from Ada and Mr. Jarndyce, she realizes that, since she has lived, heaven has decreed that she should not be punished for the circumstances of her birth.

Late the next afternoon Ada, who has not seen Esther since her illness, tearfully holds Esther's scarred face in her hands and calls her "by every tender name she could think of."

Comment

Esther, who has for Lady Dedlock returned from the dead, now knows completely the secret of her birth. Evil tidings are, however, twice foreshadowed - first, in Lady Dedlock's fears of Mr. Tulkinghorn; and second, in Esther's premonition on the Ghost's Walk.

CHAPTER THIRTY-SEVEN: JARNDYCE AND JARNDYCE

A week after Ada's arrival, Richard, accompanied by Harold Skimpole, sends Esther a message and meets her at the Dedlock

Arms, a local tavern. He relates his suspicions of Mr. Jarndyce as an "interested party" in Jarndyce and Jarndyce, seeks her help in convincing Ada of the justice of his position. Reluctantly, Esther takes him to Ada, with whom he attempts "in the most ingenious way to justify himself." Later, in a letter Ada reject his suit, and reminds him that he is "quite free" to pursue is chosen way.

The next day Richard, seeking further assistance from Esther, reveals that he has engaged the services of a "legal advisor," a Mr. Vholes, "a sallow man with pinched lips," first introduced to Richard by Skimpole for a "commission" of few pounds. It is immediately apparent to Esther that Richard has surrounded himself with two birds of prey - first, with the conscienceless Skimpole, and now with the opportunistic Vholes, who sees in Richard an "opportunity" to leave his three daughters some "independence."

Comment

Richard's involvement in Jarndyce and Jarndyce is now complete. Like so many others in the past, he is blind to the greed of those who pretend to help him.

CHAPTER THIRTY-EIGHT: A STRUGGLE

A few days after her return to Bleak House, Esther makes a short stay in London. She visits Caddy Jellyby, whom she discovers busily engaged in taking care of old Mr. Turveydrop, whose comfort has apparently increased immeasurably by the addition of Caddy to the family. Although it is obvious that Caddy's is a "laborious life," Caddy assures Esther that she is happy and that she is no longer her mother's "impolite and inky" secretary.

Later, with Caddy, Esther goes to the home of Guppy in Old Road Street where they are greeted by old Mrs. Guppy, a lady with an unsteady eye and a red nose who smiles incessantly, and Guppy, who seems embarrassed and amazed at the change which illness has wrought in Esther. Explaining that she now possesses all the information about herself that she wishes, Esther prevails upon Guppy to abandon his investigation of her past. In exchange for this favor, Esther carefully, in the most proper legal terminology, releases him from his proposal of marriage with Caddy as witness - a release which the grateful and relieved Mr. Guppy, promising in exchange "bowers of friendship," finds necessary to be twice repeated.

Comment

Esther's meeting with Guppy not only eliminates him as a suitor, but serves as kind of comic relief from the serious events of the preceding chapters.

CHAPTER THIRTY-NINE: ATTORNEY AND CLIENT

In a small, stale, and unpainted office in Symond's Inn, Chancery Lane, Mr. Vholes and Richard sit discussing the recent Chancery session at which Richard despondently feels nothing has been accomplished. Mr. Vholes replies to this in a seemingly endless series of cliches, saying that "a great deal is doing" and he urges Richard to acquire some of his own "insensibility." After reminding Richard of his good fortune in having a representative who devotes his entire professional "interest" to Richard's "problems," he has the confused Richard sign another draft to pay the "costs" of his professional services.

Guppy and Weevle watch the brooding Richard as he leaves Vholes' office and Weevle comments, "There's combustion going on there! It's not a case of spontaneous, but it's smoldering combustion, it is." For Richard is slowly being consumed, as are all the victims of Chancery.

Then, resuming the conversation that was interrupted by Richard's appearance, Guppy tells Weevle that their partnership is dissolved, since he has no further interest in Esther, and the two proceed to Krook's shop to remove Weevle's belongings. Here they discover the Smallweeds, directed by Grandfather Smallweed, delving into the still enormous litter of the Bottle Shop while Mr. Tulkinghorn looks on in amazement, still seeking evidence of Lady Dedlock's involvement with Mr. Nemo.

Comment

Dust and wastepaper are familiar Dickens symbols for the dirt and wastefulness which are the visible product of industrialism, and of a society whose charity is, like Mrs. Jellybys', a long, useless series of correspondences. They are, finally, symbols of Chancery, a legal system based on outmoded precedents, whose product is human waste and suffering.

CHAPTER FORTY: NATIONAL AND DOMESTIC

Chesney Wold is again filled with innumerable cousins awaiting news of Sir Leicester's anticipated victory in the national elections. As usual, the Doodles and the Noodles of the aristocracy have thrown themselves upon the country - "chiefly in the form of sovereign and beer," and even Sir Leicester bemoans, to Volumnia Dedlock, the expense of "hundreds of thousands of pounds to the party," although it is "whispered abroad that these expenses will be unpleasantly connected with the word 'bribery'."

Finally, Mr. Tulkinghorn arrives and as Lady Dedlock sits quietly on one side, announces Sir Leicester's crushing defeat at the hands of the opposition led by Mr. Rouncewell and his son Watt. In a general outburst of indignation, Sir Leicester remarks that the "floodgates of society are burst open," a remark variously echoed by the cousins as "votes-giv'n-mob," and "country's going -Dayvle [Devil]."

Mr. Tulkinghorn then proceeds to tell a pointed story about a lady who had once been engaged to an army captain and had born him an illegitimate child. The same lady had lately been attracted to the daughter of a man like Rouncewell because the girl reminded her of her own lost child, but the lady's secret was finally revealed by an "imprudence on her own part" and the girl's father had her removed from the lady's company.

Comment

Dickens comments strongly on the election procedures of the nineteenth century in which it was common for electors to be bribed, and the vote of a Rotten Borough (see glossary) used to secure victory.

CHAPTER FORTY-ONE: IN MR. TULKINGHORN'S ROOM

Visited in his turret room by the frightened and disturbed Lady Dedlock, Tulkinghorn unemotionally tells her that he knows all. Afraid that he will expose her, she offers to leave

Chesney Wold "tonight" if he will promise to spare Rosa from disgrace. But Mr. Tulkinghorn, unable to decide quite what to do at the moment, insists that Lady Dedlock stay for the sake of Sir Leicester, promising only that he will not reveal anything without first informing her. Shaken, Lady Dedlock is forced to agree.

Comment

Lady Dedlock is now completely at the mercy of the unfeeling and almost inhuman Tulkinghorn, the representative of an equally unfeeling and inhuman legal machinery.

CHAPTER FORTY-TWO: IN MR. TULKINGHORN'S CHAMBERS

After returning to his chambers in Lincoln's Inn, Mr. Tulkinghorn is visited by Mr. Snagsby, who informs him that his "domestic happiness" is being hard pressed by the constant "hovering" around his establishment of a "foreign female" (Hortense), seeking Mr. Tulkinghorn. Citing the "excitableness" of his "little woman," and the fact that "the foreigner's looks - which are fierce," are sending poor Guster into fits, he plaintively appeals to Mr. Tulkinghorn for help. Mr. Tulkinghorn apologizes to Mr. Snagsby for any inconvenience and requests simply that if Hortense appears again she be sent to him.

Almost immediately after Snagsby's departure, Hortense appears and angrily accuses Mr. Tulkinghorn of falsely securing her help in verifying Lady Dedlock's visit to Nemo's grave. Although she feels that she had not been fully paid, she offers to further aid Mr. Tulkinghorn in order to "disgrace and dishonor"

Lady Dedlock, whom she hates. When Mr. Tulkinghorn refuses her demand that he find her a "good condition" (a job), she violently threatens to return "and yet again, forever." Calmly, Mr. Tulkinghorn replies with his own threat of having her imprisoned if she should return, and she leaves, still muttering threats.

Comment

As cats and birds are traditional enemies, so are the crowlike Tulkinghorn and the feline Hortense. This, of course, is Dickens' subtle way of **foreshadowing** the result of their relationship.

CHAPTER FORTY-THREE: ESTHER'S NARRATIVE

In numerous conversations with Mr. Jarndyce on the subject of Richard, Esther and Ada attempt to convince him that Richard is fast becoming the victim of the "childlike" Skimpole. Although at first Mr. Jarndyce refuses to believe that so "uncalculating a creature" could influence anyone, he is determined to speak to Skimpole when informed that Skimpole has introduced Vholes to Richard for a "present" of five pounds.

Accordingly, they all go to Skimpole's place, called the Polygon, in Somers Town, where they find Skimpole lying on a sofa, amid the almost unbelievable squalor of his dilapidated home, "looking at a collection of wallflowers on the balcony." As usual, Skimpole claims to have no idea of time or money, pictures himself as a man who admires "people who possess practical wisdom," and asks for his family and himself, "to let us live upon you." Then, after introducing his wife, to whom Mr. Jarndyce quietly gives money, and his "roses" (daughters), he announces his intention of returning with them to Bleak House in order to escape the visit of an angry baker whose furniture he has borrowed and "worn out."

Shortly after their arrival at Bleak House, they are surprised by a visit from Sir Leicester Dedlock, who has stopped on his way to Lincolnshire to apologize for the fact that his difficulties with Mr.

Boythorn have prevented their visiting Chesney Wold while they were in Lincolnshire. Surprised and pleased too is Harold Skimpole, who earns Sir Leicester's approval when he confesses himself" a perfectly idle man" who is properly grateful for such "public benefactors" as Sir Leicester.

Later Esther, fearing that she may again be brought into contact with Lady Dedlock, seeks Mr. Jarndyce's advice. When he reveals that Lady Dedlock's sister had once been the intended wife of Mr. Boythorn, "a wife who did not die but died to him," Esther feels impelled to tell him that she has not only seen that lady (Miss Barbary) many times, but that Lady Dedlock is her mother.

Comment

Mr. Boythorn is revealed to be a person also involved in the mystery of Esther's past. Thus, each of the novel's major characters serves some function in the working out of the complicated plot.

CHAPTER FORTY-FOUR: THE LETTER AND THE ANSWER

The following morning Esther reveals to Mr. Jarndyce the remaining facts that she had learned of her past, and expresses her fears for Lady Dedlock from the prying Mr. Tulkinghorn and the vindictive Hortense. Calming her fears, Mr. Jarndyce counsels her to reveal to no one what she knows. He then explains that there is something that he has long wished to say, something so serious that he preferred to write it in a letter. Only when Esther has expressed her complete trust in him, does he arrange for the letter, which was already written, to be delivered to her by Charley.

The letter contains a proposal of marriage, stated in the kindest of terms, and reveals Mr. Jarndyce's awareness of the disadvantage which age would pose for such a marriage, but declares his love and a willingness to accept gladly whatever answer Esther may give.

Greatly moved by the letter, Esther cries until her eyes are red and swollen, aware of how much the kindly Mr. Jarndyce loves her, in spite of the disfigurement caused by her recent illness, and the facts which she had revealed to him about her birth. Then, remembering some flowers which Mr. Woodcourt left, and which she has so carefully saved, she tearfully burns them. Finally, after almost a week of waiting for Mr. Jarndyce to speak of the letter, Esther returns it to him and tells him that her answer is "Yes."

Comment

While Mr. Jarndyce's proposal is not a totally unexpected plot development, it does come as something of a surprise to the reader. Since the mystery which surrounded Esther's birth has finally been revealed, this new development is needed to maintain the reader's interest in her. Now the reader is concerned for her future.

BLEAK HOUSE

CHAPTER FORTY-FIVE: IN TRUST

One morning Mr. Vholes, Richard's lawyer, arrives unexpectedly at Bleak House and, hinting broadly that Richard's debts to him are considerable, seeks to discover Richard's true financial position. Although he disclaims any interest, except Richard's, he is careful to tell Esther "not to refer to me, Miss, in communicating with Mr. C. [Richard Carstone]."

Since Richard is in obvious need of assistance, Esther, accompanied by Charley leaves for Deal, a seaport town, where Richard is preparing for his army career abroad. Here they discover Richard on the verge of resigning his commission in order to further pursue his interests in Jarndyce and Jarndyce. Already in disgrace with his superiors, he cannot be persuaded to change his mind, so Esther gives him a letter from Ada which she has brought with her. After Richard reads it, he tells Esther that it contains an offer from Ada to give him "the little inheritance she is certain of." Interpreting it as another means of buying him off, Richard angrily refuses. Since nothing can be done, Esther offers to wait at her hotel until he is free from the army, and then accompany him back to London.

Returning to her hotel by way of the waterfront, Esther recognizes Mr. Allan Woodcourt among a group of officers disembarking from a boat. When the officers come to the hotel where she was staying, Esther determines to inform him of her presence, and he comes immediately. First congratulating him on his heroism, she gives him all the news he requires about Miss Flite, Richard, and herself. Mr. Woodcourt, realizing Richard's plight, kindly offers to befriend him in London, and do what he can to help. Finally, Richard arrives and leaves with Esther and Charley for London.

Comment

In the accidental meeting between Esther and Mr. Woodcourt, coincidence is again employed to advance the plot.

CHAPTER FORTY-SIX: STOP HIM!

In spite of all the political activity in England because of the elections, nothing has changed in Tom-All-Alone's street. The contagion and pollution that it transmits affect every level of English society from the "highest of the high" to those unfortunates sleeping in cold doorways.

One of those sleepers is Jenny (the brickmaker's wife), who has wandered through the streets all night in search of lodging after a beating at the hands of her drunken husband. Allan

Woodcourt, finding her, treats her wounds and offers her money for lodging.

After leaving her, Allan sees the same woman chasing a boy (Jo), and although he is not aware of her reason, he joins in the chase and helps her capture him. Jenny only wishes to thank Jo for the help which he had given when Liz's child was ill, and to find out why he had run away when Esther had taken him to Bleak House to help him when he was ill. Allan secures from the tearful and frightened Jo the information that he had been "took away" from Bleak House by Mr. Bucket and sent to a hospital, and after he was discharged from the hospital given money and told "to move on," to get far away from London. Since it is now nearly daylight, Allan takes Jo with him to find him a place to stay, and Jenny goes on her way.

Comment

Allan Woodcourt becomes more deeply involved in the plot. Almost immediately after his chance meeting with Esther, he "accidentally" meets Jo and decides to help him.

CHAPTER FORTY-SEVEN: JO'S WILL

Attempting to find lodging for the fearful and sick Jo, Allan Woodcourt seeks out Miss Flite, who is now living with Mrs. Blinder in Bell yard where she occupies poor Gridley's room. She suggests that perhaps "General George" (George Rouncewell) will help out, and they go to the shooting gallery where George, after hearing the name Bucket, relates his own difficulties with Tulkinghorn and offers to take Jo in. Unlike Mrs. Pardiggle and Mrs. Jellyby, George and his assistant, Phil Squod, practice their charity not on the "genuine foreign-grown savage ... softened by distance," but on the "ordinary home-made article," dirty, ugly, and disagreeable, as exemplified by Jo.

Having now accidentally discovered, through Jo and George Rouncewell, Mr. Tulkinghorn's interest in Esther's past, Allan goes to see Mr. Jarndyce, to whom he relates this information. As they return to talk with Jo, Mr. Jarndyce confides that "there are reasons for keeping this matter very quiet indeed." A few days later, since Jo's condition is growing worse, Allan seeks out Mr. Snagsby, whom Jo has referred in his conversation, and returns with him to the shooting gallery. Here the kindly Mr. Snagsby, still much affected by his wife's suspicion, reveals the warning that he has received (from Mr. Tulkinghorn) not to speak of Jo to anyone, and gives Jo two half crowns. Later, as Jo's condition grows worse, he speaks of his frightened and confused life, and finally, since he knows that he is soon going to die, requests that he be buried in the "berrin ground" near Mr. Nemo. At last, with his hand in Allan's, he dies quietly.

Comment

The death of poor Jo is an example of Dickens' many famous moving, pathetic death scenes.

CHAPTER FORTY EIGHT: CLOSING IN

Chesney Wold is again closed for the season, as the Dedlocks are in London busy receiving people of fashion, while the ever present Mr. Tulkinghorn looks ominously on. Finally, Lady Dedlock, unable to stand the strain of Mr. Tulkinghorn's threat, decides to throw it off. However, she must first provide for Rosa's future, so she pretends that Rosa has been an annoyance to her because of her love for young Watt. She sends for Mr. Rouncewell, the ironmaster. In a scene in which she observes that Rosa has been "insensible to her advantages," Mr. Rouncewell is persuaded to take Rosa away with him.

Mr. Tulkinghorn shrewdly suspects Lady Dedlock's reason for Rosa's dismissal and reminds her that, according to their agreement, he is now free to betray her to Sir Leicester any time he wishes, without any advance notice.

Later, Mr. Tulkinghorn returns home to his dull room where a shot is heard. The next morning he is found lying face down with a bullet through his heart.

Comment

In succeeding chapters Dickens has devised death scenes of vastly different types. Poor Jo, whose life has been filled with pain and frustration, dies serenely, and the cold and devious lawyer is mysteriously and violently murdered. Even the manner of the death of his characters is appropriate and characteristic.

CHAPTER FORTY-NINE: DUTIFUL FRIENDSHIP

The great annual occasion at the Bagnets' is Mrs. Bagnet's birthday. Each year on this day, Mr. Bagnet brings home two fowls which he then proceeds to cook to almost inedible toughness and which he and the children serve with great fanfare. At precisely four-thirty, which is "military time," they all sit down to dinner and another old soldier, George Rouncewell, arrives.

As the Bagnets listen while George sadly relates the news of Jo's death, and Mrs. Bagnet offers him a pipe by way of comfort and consolation, they are interrupted by a visit from Mr. Bucket (the detective whom Mr. Tulkinghorn had hired). Pretending that he was drawn to the shop by the musical instruments in the window, Bucket, making much of the Bagnet children, manages to get himself invited to the party. Agreeable and friendly to George throughout the afternoon, Bucket accompanies him when he leaves, and, leading him in friendly fashion to the parlor of a public house nearby, announces suddenly that he is taking George into "custody" for the murder of Mr. Tulkinghorn. Later, he secures from the astonished George the admission that he had been in Lincoln's Inn on the evening of the murder. Then a bit ashamed of what he has done, Bucket attempts to justify his actions to George by arguing that he is merely doing his duty and that he as well as another might as well collect the hundred-guinea reward offered by Sir Leicester Dedlock. He then leads the cloaked and handcuffed George off to jail.

Comment

Inspector Bucket, like so many others who pretend to do good, always feels obliged to explain away the guilt feelings accompanying acts that bring to others, as duty or responsibility rather than self-interest.

CHAPTER FIFTY: ESTHER'S NARRATIVE

Soon after her arrival from Deal, Esther receives a letter from Caddy Jellyby, informing her that she is now a mother, but that she is very ill and needs Esther's help. Esther then makes daily trips to London to care for Caddy until Mr. Jarndyce, afraid that these trips are too strenuous, suggests that they all (Esther, Ada, and he) go to London to stay for a while, and that Mr. Woodcourt be called to confirm the opinion of Caddy's present doctor. Attended by Mr. Woodcourt, under the solicitous care of Esther, Mrs. Jellyby, and old Mr. Turveydrop, Caddy soon begins to improve.

As Caddy improves, Esther begins to notice a change in Ada who has become quiet and withdrawn. Sensing that perhaps Ada's sadness is due to worry about Richard, or to Esther's engagement to Mr. Jarndyce, Esther attempts to draw her out, but Ada finds what she wants to say too difficult to tell. Meanwhile, Mr. Jarndyce finds himself much attracted to Mr. Woodcourt in whom he fancies he sees "some particular disappointment or misfortune."

Comment

Ada is actually keeping a secret which will be revealed in the next chapter.

CHAPTER FIFTY-ONE: ENLIGHTENED

Because of his promise to Esther, immediately after arriving in London Allan Woodcourt goes to Mr. Vholes' office seeking Richard. Here the wily Vholes, aware of Allan's obvious interest in Richard, hints strongly that, if Richard expects to win his Chancery suit, more money will be needed. Although he, as usual, disclaims any personal interest in the matter, he is careful to point out that his own responsibility to his aged father and his three daughters prevents him from taking too great a financial risk on Richard's behalf. Finally, Allan discovers Richard living in a dull, badly furnished room next door to Mr. Vholes' office. Here the haggard and dejected Richard greets Allan warmly, accepts his proffered friendship, and reminds Allan of his great attachment for Ada.

Meanwhile, Esther accompanied by Ada, visits Richard in his room in Symmond's Inn, where Ada reveals that she and Richard have been secretly married for two months. The surprised Esther, feeling both joy and pity at their difficult situation, blesses them both and wishes them well. After she leaves, she cries and later that evening informs Mr. Jarndyce, who also is greatly saddened by the news and by the fact that Bleak House is "thinning fast." Esther, too, begins to feel that she is not all that she had meant to be to Mr. Jarndyce since she had accepted his proposal of marriage.

Comment

Mr. Jarndyce's presentiment that Bleak House is "thinning fast" is a hint of other changes to come, as are Esther's second thoughts on his proposal of marriage.

CHAPTER FIFTY-TWO: OBSTINACY

Two days later, Allan Woodcourt arrives at Bleak House with the news of Mr. Tulkinghorn's murder and the fact that George Rouncewell is now in custody, accused of the murder. Surprised and distressed at the news, neither Esther nor Mr. Jarndyce finds it possible to believe that so "open-hearted and compassionate" a man as George could have committed such a crime. Accordingly they immediately go to the prison to offer him their help. Here, the soldierly George coolly informs them of his innocence and his determination to defend himself with "the truth." Having already had a number of unfortunate encounters with lawyers, he refuses their offer of a lawyer because he "object[s] to the breed [lawyers] who "quibble" and resort to distortions to free their clients, rather than relying openly on the truth.

At this point Mr. and Mrs. Bagnet arrive, bearing a basket of food, but they too fail in an attempt to persuade the determined George to change his mind. Later, Mrs. Bagnet informs Mr. Jarndyce and Esther that she knows that George's mother (Mrs. Rouncewll, the Dedlock's housekeeper) is alive and immediately set off to Lincolnshire to bring her back.

Comment

George, of course, knew that his mother was alive, but had never informed her that he was alive because he felt himself to be a failure.

CHAPTER FIFTY-THREE: THE TRACK

As Mr. Bucket pursues his investigation into the death of Mr. Tulkinghorn, the noble and fashionable attend Mr. Tulkinghorn's funeral. Assisted by Mrs. Bucket, who is currently watching Mr. Tulkinghorn's house, Mr. Bucket is attempting to discover the identity of the person who has been sending him anonymous letters containing only the words "Lady Dedlock." At the moment, on good terms with Sir Leicester, whose reward he has received, Mr. Bucket cleverly questions Volumnia Dedlock, Lady Dedlock, and "Mercury" (the Dedlock's footman). From the latter he secures the information that on the evening of the murder, Lady Dedlock left the London house at 9:30 through the garden.

Comment

Although Mr. Tulkinghorn is no longer a threat to Lady Dedlock, the threat reappears in the guise of Mr. Bucket.

CHAPTER FIFTY-FOUR: SPRINGING A MINE

The morning after the funeral, Mr. Bucket reveals privately to Sir Leicester the results of his investigation. He relates to the shocked and angry Sir Leicester, Mr. Tulkinghorn's suspicion and investigation of Lady Dedlock and the fact that Lady Dedlock was present at Mr. Tulkinghorn's at the same time as George Rouncewell on the evening of the murder.

As Bucket suggests that Sir Leicester question Lady Dedlock on these matters, they are interrupted by a number of visitors including Grandfather Smallweed, Mr. and Mr. Chadband, and Mrs. Snagsby. Each appears to have information concerning Lady Dedlock's secret, and now that Mr. Tulkinghorn is dead, they have come to deal directly with Sir Leicester. At Bucket's urging, Sir Leicester allows him to handle the visitors and he secures from each of them the information he possesses.

Mr. Smallweed has come, seeking the letters which he gave to Mr. Tulkinghorn revealing the relationship between Captain Hawdon (Nemo) and Lady Dedlock, and his price for silence is five hundred pounds. Mrs. Chadband tells that she helped to raise Lady Dedlock's daughter by Captain Hawdon, a child who is still alive and living nearby. Finally, Mrs. Snagsby relates that as a result of her suspicions of her husband, whom she has followed relentlessly, she has arrived at the conclusion that Mr. Snagsby is Jo's father. Although she does not wish any money for the price of her silence, it has been her confused meddling that has brought together the Chadbands and Mr. Tulkinghorn, with the present result.

After they all leave, Mr. Bucket strongly recommends that Sir Leicester buy the silence of the group, which he believes "may be bought pretty cheap," and has Mercury bring in Hortense, whom he has kept waiting outside. He then confronts the angry and spiteful Hortense with evidence of her guilt in Mr. Tulkinghorn's murder. Suspicious of her from the moment of his arrival home after the murder (Hortense has been a lodger at the Buckets) he has watched her continuously since and knows that she is the sender of the anonymous letters and that she had disposed of the murder weapon (which Bucket had recovered) in a small lake. Bucket then triumphantly marches off with his spiteful prisoner, while the stunned and shocked Sir Leicester sits alone contemplating the blow to his dignity and pride, and thinks of the woman he still loves in spite of everything.

Comment

A climactic chapter in which the murder of Mr. Tulkinghorn is solved, and in which Sir Leicester finally discovers Lady Dedlock's guilty secret.

CHAPTER FIFTY-FIVE: FLIGHT

At Chesney Wold, Mrs. Rouncewell is overjoyed at Mrs. Bagnet's news that George is alive, and returns with her, determined to see that George receives "all the help that can be got for him." At the prison she enters George's cell alone to surprise him. They tearfully embrace for the first time in many years and, as George sobs his regrets at having been so "bad" a son, she forgives him among many tears and convinces him that he must accept legal help, although he pleads that his brother (the ironmaster) not be told.

Mrs. Rouncewell goes to the London town house of the Dedlocks, where she asks Lady Dedlock if she cares to say the words which will clear George. She then gives Lady Dedlock an anonymous letter which she has received, containing a printed account of the finding of Mr. Tulkinghorn's body, under which were inscribed the words "Lady Dedlock-Murderess," and asks that Lady Dedlock read it after she has left. Although she does not wish to hurt Lady Dedlock, Mrs. Rouncewell's love for her son has overcome any other consideration.

Almost immediately after she has read the letter, Lady Dedlock is visited by Guppy, who informs her that others now possess the letters which he had sought to get for her, and that they have undoubtedly already approached Sir Leicester with the information for the purpose of blackmail. Discovering from Mercury that strangers of the same description have already been to see Sir Leicester, Lady Dedlock, fearing that she will now be accused of murder, writes a farewell note to Sir Leicester in which she tells him that she is innocent (of Mr. Tulkinghorn's murder), but that she wishes to spare him any further shame. She then dresses quickly and runs out into the cold and windy night.

Comment

The melodramatic use of coincidence is used here almost to the breaking point. For example Mrs. Rouncewell's arrival followed almost immediately by Mr. Guppy's each supplying Lady Dedlock with frightening and dramatic news.

CHAPTER FIFTY-SIX: PURSUIT

Sir Leicester Dedlock is discovered by Volumnia, lying on the floor in the London town house in a serious state of shock, and although hours later he is able to nod or move his hand, he is unable to speak. Fortunately, Mrs. Rouncewell arrives and perceives that he wants a slate. She tells him that he is ill, in London, and that Lady Dedlock has run away. When Sir Leicester writes "B" on the slate, Mrs. Rouncewell guesses that he wants Mr. Bucket, so he is brought and immediately sent after Lady Dedlock, to whom Sir Leicester offers full forgiveness.

After a search of Lady Dedlock's room for clues to her whereabouts, Mr. Bucket is able to find only Esther's handkerchief (which Lady Dedlock had gotten from Jenny), so he goes to George Rouncewell (now back at his shooting gallery) and gets, from him, Esther's address at Bleak House. Here, showing Mr. Jarndyce Lady Dedlock's farewell note, and convincing him that delay may be "dangerous," he secures permission for Esther to accompany him on his search.

Meanwhile, Lady Dedlock wanders near the brick kilns (St. Alban's section) "pelted by the snow, and driven by the wind, cast out it would seem from all companionship."

Comment

Although much of the novel's **climax** is revealed, interest is maintained through an urgent search for Lady Dedlock, who in her desperate state, may harm herself.

CHAPTER FIFTY-SEVEN: ESTHER'S NARRATIVE

Awakened by Mr. Jarndyce and informed of Lady Dedlock's flight, Esther joins Mr. Bucket in the search. They first go to a police station, where they secure a carriage, and set out through London, towards St. Albans, past Bleak House, in search of Harold Skimpole, whom Mr. Bucket had sometime before given a five-pound note in exchange for information about Jo. It is obvious to Esther that Mr. Bucket does not like Skimpole, whom he feels to be a fraud.

Unable to locate Skimpole, they proceed to the brickmaker's cottage where Mr. Bucket discovers that Lady Dedlock was there on the previous night for an hour or two, and that she had left with Jenny, who went to London while Lady Dedlock went the other way. They then resume their relentless pursuit until Esther faints from exhaustion, and they have to pause at an inn to refresh themselves and wait for Esther to recover. Resuming the chase after only a half-hour rest, they have not gone far when Mr. Bucket, who has been pondering the story which they had gotten from Liz, since they left the cottage, suddenly orders the stage to turn about and make all speed for London, asking Esther only to "rely" on him.

Comment

This chapter is filled with all of the excitement of the chase. Hampered by bad weather, Esther and Bucket secure a slim lead, but Bucket suspects that they have been misdirected.

CHAPTER FIFTY-EIGHT: A WINTRY DAY AND NIGHT

Back in London, gossip has already begun to spread about Lady Dedlock's disappearance. While unaware of these developments, Sir Leicester, his pain dulled by opiates, anxiously awaits some news. Overhearing Mrs. Rouncewell mention that her son George, who was long thought dead, has returned home, Sir Dedlock recovers his speech dramatically and requests that George be brought to him. Reminded then by George's presence, of years gone by at Chesney Wold, Sir Leicester is heartened and a pretense is maintained that Lady Dedlock will be returning shortly. Thus attended by George, Mrs. Rouncewell, and Volumnia (who is concerned about her income - should "anything happen" to Sir Leicester), he waits the return of Lady Dedlock. Finally, George escorts the exhausted Volumnia to her bed and maintains his vigil over Sir Leicester throughout the long night.

Comment

At last George Rouncewell has come home, and Sir Leicester Dedlock, who defends Lady Dedlock to Volumnia, becomes a man, rather than just a noble caricature.

CHAPTER FIFTY-NINE: ESTHER'S NARRATIVE

Returning through the cold and sleeting night, Esther and Mr. Bucket meet Allan Woodcourt, returning home after a visit to Richard, who, he explains, is "not quite well." Allan then accompanies them to Mr. Snagsbys, where he seeks Guster, the Snagsby servant. Since Guster is having one of her violent fits (which she always has when pressed), Mr. Bucket asks for Mr. Woodcourt's assistance while he strongly informs Mrs. Snagsby that her suspicion of her husband are foolish, and berates her for pouncing on poor Guster and producing a violent fit, especially since he believes that "a life may be hanging on that girl's words." Explaining that Mr. Snagsby's involvement with Jo is only the result of his business with Mr. Tulkinhorn, he then accuses Mrs. Snagsby of pouncing on Guster because she has, last evening, observed a mysterious paper pass between Guster and a wretchedly dressed lady (Lady Dedlock).

He then secures a letter, addressed to Esther Summerson, which poor Guster has been unable to deliver because of her fit. It relates, in portions obviously written at different times by Esther's mother, that she has gotten the help of the brickmakers in her attempt to escape.

Later she wandered for many hours, cold and wet, feeling that she deserved to die because of her guilt, and finally, in words apparently written in the darkness, she begs forgiveness and bids farewell.

Turning back to Guster, Mr. Bucket secures from her the information that she had shown the Lady to the burying ground (where Mr. Nemo was buried), and they all hurry to that awful place. Here, lying on a step at the gate, they discover what Esther believed to be the body of Jenny, the brickmaker's wife. Restrained by Allan, she listens uncomprehendingly while Mr. Bucket explains that Lady Dedlock and Jenny changed clothes at the cottage in order for Lady Dedlock to escape her pursuers. Allowed finally to go forward, she discovers that it is not Jenny but her mother, "cold and dead."

Comment

In this chapter the **foreshadowing** of death and disgrace in the footsteps in Chesney Wold's famous Ghost's Walk is finally realized.

CHAPTER SIXTY: PERSPECTIVE

Mr. Jarndyce, determined to help Richard and Ada despite their estrangement, has decided to remain in London. Here, with the help of Esther and Mr. Woodcourt, he hopes that Richard will recover from the malady of Jarndyce and Jarndyce, which has so affected his mind and health, and which is now destroying Ada as well.

Staying with Esther and Mr. Jarndyce at their London lodgings, is Mrs. Woodcourt, who recently nursed Esther through the illness brought on by the death of her mother. As a result, it is natural that Mr. Woodcourt often visits them and that Esther and Mr. Jarndyce discuss Allan Woodcourt, whom he is advising on his career. He tells her that Allan hopes to secure an appointment which will soon be open in a small Yorkshire town. He was certain that, although the appointment will mean a "great amount of work and a small amount of pay," Allan will prosper. Esther replies "that the place would have reason to bless the choice, if it falls on Mr. Woodcourt."

Esther often goes to visit Ada and Richard, and on these occasions Richard is either absent (probably at the Chancery Court), or pouring over endless heaps of paper on a table. When he is not occupied with either of these diversions, he can be found lounging about the neighborhood, worriedly biting his nails. With Ada's small fortune now also melting away, he is growing "poorer and poorer every day." It is on one of these visits that Esther meets Miss Elite who ominously reports that, with poor Gridley (the man from Shropshire) gone, Richard is now her executor.

On another occasion, Esther meets the unscrupulous Mr. Vholes, who, during a momentary absence from the room of Ada and Richard, assures her that although he felt Richard's marriage was very ill-advised, he is still doing everything he can in the pursuit of Richard's "interests." Unfortunately, the now thin and languid Richard seems to share Mr. Vhole's belief about the pursuit of his "interest," so that even the good influence of Mr. Woodcourt, who also comes to dinner that day, is only temporary.

After Richard and Allan have gone out for a walk, Ada confides to Esther that she is about to have a child, whom she hopes will restore Richard to his senses. However, Ada is greatly afraid that in his present condition Richard "may not live to see his child."

Comment

Again the last few lines of the chapter are a **foreshadowing** of what is to come. Ada's suggestion that Richard may not live is all too true. Also significant is Miss Elite's appointment of Richard, (as much a victim of Chancery as poor Mr. Gridley), as her executor.

BLEAK HOUSE

CHAPTERS 61–67 AND CHARACTER ANALYSIS

. . . .

CHAPTER SIXTY-ONE: A DISCOVERY

On her visits to Richard and Ada, Esther often meets Harold Skimpole, idly playing the piano and exerting his harmful influence on Richard. Disturbed by that influence, Esther leaves with "Charley" for Somers Town, in an effort to persuade Skimpole to stay away. Surprisingly he agrees cheerful, admitting the Richard and Ada are losing their "youthful poetry which was so captivating" (and incidentally also losing their money). Since they are now reduced to "prose," any association with them can only produce in him pain rather than the pleasure which he always sought. Even more surprising is his answer to Esther's accusation that he accepted a bribe from Mr. Bucket for betraying Jo. To this he answers that since he never attached any value to money, nothing he received could possibly be described as a bribe, and in any case the fault, if there is one, belongs to the intelligent and clever Mr. Bucket. Although Esther never again sees Mr. Skimpole, she relates that a coolness grows between him and Mr. Jarndyce because Skimpole disregarded Mr. Jarndyce's entreaties to stay away from Richard. At the death of Skimpole about five years later, he leaves a diary and some other papers to be published containing the ungrateful comment that Mr. Jarndyce "is the incarnation of selfishness."

As the months pass, Richard grows more and more worn and haggard in spite of everything that Esther and Allan Woodcourt try to do. As a result of these common efforts, Esther and Allan are often thrown together and on one of these occasions Allan tells Esther that he loves her. Although Esther feels great joy in his confession, she cannot, because of her promise to Mr. Jarndyce (to whom she owes so much), encourage his love.

Comment

Esther's obligation to Mr. Jarndyce is a variation of the parental objection device often used by novelists as a barrier between lovers. As is usually the case, it will soon be removed so that the path of true love may run smooth.

CHAPTER SIXTY-TWO: ANOTHER DISCOVERY

The next morning after breakfast, Esther speaks to Mr. Jarndyce about their engagement, and they decide to be married within the next month. Almost immediately, Mr. Bucket arrives with Mr. Smallweed in tow, to inform them that Smallweed has discovered, among the rubbish of Mr. Krook's shop, a new Jarndyce will. Mr. Bucket then makes the reluctant Mr. Smallweed turn the new will over to Mr. Jarndyce, who, although he is thoroughly sick of Jarndyce and Jarndyce and refuses to look at it, declares that the will shall be immediately turned over to his solicitors (Kenge and Carboy) to determine its value. He promises to reward the greedy Mr. Smallweed if it should prove of any value.

Later Mr. Kenge, realizing that the will bears a date later than any in the suit at present, predicts that it is the "perfect instrument" for the solution of the suit, an opinion repeated later by Mr. Vholes. They then begin preparations for that settlement at the next Chancery term which is to begin in a month.

Comment

Although Jarndyce and Jarndyce at last nears a conclusion, it is doubtful whether there will be much of the estate left.

CHAPTER SIXTY-THREE: STEEL AND IRON

Having sold his shooting gallery, George Rouncewell is now back at Chesney Wold, where he is attending Sir Leicester. From here, one day, he travels north into the iron country to visit his brother, the ironmaster, and with him he shares a joyous reunion. Overwhelmed by his brother's welcome, and surprised by the invitation to be the guest of honor at Watt and Rosa's wedding, which will be held when she returns after a year's study in Germany, George feels more than ever that he is the family "scapegrace," and hopes that his mother will "scratch" him from her will. Although his brother persuades him that such a drastic action is neither desirable nor necessary, he refuses the ironmaster's offer of a job because he is "kind of a weed, and it's too late to plant me in a regular garden." He prefers instead to serve Sir Leicester Dedlock at Chesney Wold, where he feels more at home.

George then shows his brother a letter which he has written to Esther in which he explains that the letter that he had been forced to give to Mr. Tulkinghorn had only contained instructions from Captain Hawdon for the delivery of still another letter to a "young and beautiful, then unmarried lady" in England (Esther's mother). He then goes on to explain that had he known that Captain Hawdon was still alive (as Nemo) he would have "shared my last farthing with him."

Assured by his brother that the letter is adequate, George mails it and prepares to depart the next morning for Chesney Wold.

Comment

Here again we have Dickens' use of another melodramatic device. George has in a way "returned from the dead," and is now joyfully reunited with his family.

CHAPTER SIXTY-FOUR: ESTHER'S NARRATIVE

As the date for the new Chancery term and for Esther's wedding which was to follow approaches, Mr. Jarndyce suddenly goes to Yorkshire on some business for Mr. Woodcourt. From there he sends a letter requesting that Esther come immediately. When she arrives, he explains that he has purchased a suitable house for Allan, but that it needs Esther's touch as housekeeper to make it "habitable." The next day, after showing her and Allan the house and garden, Mr. Jarndyce takes them to the front porch over which he has had inscribed the words Bleak House. He then tells them that he knows how Allan and she feel about each other and releases her from her promise, reminding her that he is still going to keep his promise to make her mistress of Bleak House.

Upon their return home, Esther and Mr. Jarndyce are surprised to discover that Guppy has called three times. When he arrives with his mother and Mr. Weevle (Tony Jobling) on his fourth visit, they listen amazed as he again proposes marriage to Esther, now that he has "completed his articles" and is "on the roll of attorneys." Esther watches in amusement as Mr. Jarndyce ejects the astonished and indignant Guppy and mother, who are unable to understand Esther's rejection of the proposal.

Comment

In the closing chapters of the novel, Dickens gathers up the loose ends of the plot. In the previous chapter the Rouncewells are provided for, and now the foolish but well-meaning Guppy is launched in his career.

CHAPTER SIXTY-FIVE: BEGINNING THE WORLD

Esther and Allan go to Westminster Hall, where the case of Jarndyce and Jarndyce is to have its final hearing. But since they arrive late, they have to wait outside for news of what has happened. Finally, they are informed by Mr. Kenge and Mr. Vholes that, indeed, that "monument of Chancery practice" has at last reached a conclusion. Any hopes that they might have entertained for Richard and Ada are soon dashed, however, by Mr. Kenge's doleful legal explanation that the case has not been settled because of the introduction of the new will, but that the suit has "lapsed and melted away," because there is no more money in the estate. It had all been absorbed in legal costs.

Later, visiting Richard, who has been taken violently ill at the suit's conclusion, they realize that he is now seriously ill. As he lies on the couch, he tearfully begs Mr. Jarndyce's forgiveness, and says that he has learned a "hard" lesson, but that he will make it all right as soon as he is well enough to "begin the world" again. A short while later, he dies quietly in Ada's arms.

Comment

As the infamous Chancery suit comes to a close, it claims one more victim in Richard.

CHAPTER SIXTY-SIX: DOWN IN LINCOLNSHIRE

Chesney Wold is quiet now, although the dispute between Sir Leicester and Mr. Boythorn continues unabated. Each alike has suffered "in the fortune of two sisters," but Mr. Boythorn is not the man to tell him, so the quarrel goes on to the satisfaction of both. George Rouncewell, his assistant Phil, and Mrs. Rouncewell look after the ill and nearly blind Sir Leicester and his estate. The only visitors who come now to Chesney Wold are the Bagnets and their children, who come to visit George.

Meanwhile, Volumnia reads to Sir Leicester "long-winded treatises on the Buffy and Boodle question" in an effort to entertain him and to retain the annuities which he has secured for her. The cousins never come to Chesney Wold anymore, and it is much "abandoned to darkness and vacancy" now that the "passion and the pride ... have died away from the place."

Comment

Although Sir Leicester is not dead, he has already joined the innumerable ancestors entombed in Chesney Wold.

CHAPTER SIXTY-SEVEN: THE CLOSE OF ESTHER'S NARRATIVE

For seven happy years Esther has been the mistress of the new Bleak House, where she and Allan have had two daughters. Ada, with her son Richard, is now living with the kindly Mr. Jarndyce, and they often visit Esther and Allan.

Charley Neckett has married a well-to-do miller, and her sister Emma is now Esther's maid, while little Tom Neckett is apprenticed to the miller. Caddy Jellyby "is more than content" with her dancing school, although her husband is now lame and able to do very little. While Mr. Jellyby spends his evenings at Caddy's, happily escaping Mrs. Jellyby, that good lady has found a new mission "involving more correspondence than the old one." Peepy Jellyby is working in the Custom House and is doing very well, much to the delight of old Mr. Turveydrop, who is very fond of him, and who "still enjoys himself in the old manner."

Although Esther and Allan are not rich, they are happy, for they are well liked in Yorkshire and are still very much in love.

Comment

Thus Dickens neatly disposes of all the loose ends of his various plots. The drama, often full of sadness is played out, and they all live happily ever after.

BLEAK HOUSE

. . . .

Like most of Dickens' novels, *Bleak House* is filled with many memorable characters. The following list is an attempt to analyze most of these characters with reference to their relative importance to the story.

ESTHER SUMMERSON

Novel's heroine, housekeeper of Bleak House, companion to Ada Clare, ward of John Jarndyce, and long-lost daughter of Lady Dedlock. Although Dickens narrates much of *Bleak House* through the person of Esther (in order to achieve something of the immediacy of autobiography), she never quite emerges as a believable human being. Like most of Dickens' heroines, she is simply too good to be true. Generous and benevolent to the point of saintliness, she sounds altogether too much like Dickens himself. For example: her careful and detailed observation of others; and her clever appraisal of the characters of others, are not characteristics altogether believable in an inexperienced girl who was only twenty when she arrived at Bleak House.

JOHN JARNDYCE

Master of Bleak House, guardian to Esther, Richard, and Ada. As with Esther, his kindliness strains the reader's credibility. He joins a host of other of Dickens' lovable eccentrics, with his constant reference to the "East wind" which he claims brings on his rheumatism, and his "growlery" (a room to which he retires when disturbed) both of which enable him to escape ever having to say anything unpleasant. He occasionally steps out of character to voice violently Dickens' sentiments on Chancery, and to sermonize on the evils of society.

RICHARD CARSTONE

Chancery ward of John Jarndyce, fiance and later husband of Ada Clare. A good-hearted, but weak and foolish, young man whose gradual deterioration and destruction makes up Dickens most violent condemnation of Chancery. Although he is only sketchily drawn, he is as nearly a truly tragic hero as Dickens ever created, and his deterioration reveals the depth of Dickens' understanding of human nature.

ADA CLARE

Chancery ward of John Jarndyce, fiance and later, wife of Richard Carstone. Although she is an exceptionally good person, she is only slightly drawn, and her helplessness serves as a contrast to the positive and energetic goodness of Esther.

LADY HONORIA DEDLOCK

Wife of Sir Leicester Dedlock, mistress of Chesney Wold, mother of Esther Summerson. As the name Honoria implies, she is representative of that class of genteel society to whom appearances are important. Again a caricature whose outbursts (when she reveals to Esther that she is her mother, and when she runs away to die on Captain Hawdon's grave) are not in keeping with her cool and haughty nature.

SIR LEICESTER DEDLOCK

Husband of Lady Honoria Dedlock, Master of Chesney Wold. A sharply critical portrait of a representative of an outmoded and useless class of men as compared with the new class of doers (represented by Mr. Rouncewell, the Ironmaster). His fears that the lower classes will revolt, and that the country is being destroyed are only a means of intensifying Dickens' satiric portrait. He is, however, melodramatically humanized at the end of the novel, when after Lady Dedlock's flight and death, he is left paralyzed and alone.

MR. TULKINGHORN

Lawyer to the Dedlocks. A coldly impersonal, shrewd old lawyer, he represents another phase of Dickens' attack on England's dehumanized and impersonal legal system. An excellent portrait in depth of an ominous, brooding man who has no humanity and whose only interest lies in the legal machinery of which he is an agent.

MR. LAWRENCE BOYTHORN

An old school friend of John Jarndyce. A noisy but kind-hearted and honest man. Another of Dickens' ideal gentlemen; for beneath his rough exterior, beats a heart of gold.

HAROLD SKIMPOLE

Improvident artist, friend of Mr. Jarndyce. Although Skimpole was originally intended to be a humorous caricature of Dickens' friend, poet Leigh Hunt, he is gradually revealed as a parasite whose pretensions to art enable him to escape the labor which others find inevitable. Always an energetic man himself, it was impossible that Dickens could find such a person permanently attractive. Skimpole's lack of concern for others, even for the welfare of his own family, reveals him finally as a hypocrite and fraud whose "let Harold Skimpole live" expresses perfectly the attitude with which he regards the world.

JO, THE CROSSING SWEEPER

Befriended by Nemo, and later by Mr. Snagsby and Esther, he is a representative of an enormous class of unfortunates whose poverty and degradation are only made worse by a dehumanized and impersonal legal system (the Chancery, the police) and whose needs are ignored by the large class of philanthropists who can only see poverty at a distance. (Mrs. Jellyby, Mrs. Pardiggle, Mr. Quale, etc.)

GEORGE ROUNCEWELL

Younger son of Mrs. Rouncewell, Lord Leicester Dedlock's housekeeper. Another of Dickens' good men, a representative of a large number of recently returned soldiers who, after the Napoleonic Wars, were left to shift for themselves.

MR. ROUNCEWELL

The Ironmaster. An inventive, productive man who represents England's new ruling - a class of men whose wealth and power are not inherited, but earned.

WATT ROUNCEWELL

The Ironmaster's son, who like his father possesses the energy to succeed. The name Watt is significant since he is named for Wat Tyler, leader of the Peasant Revolt (1381), and for James Watt (1736–1819), inventor of the steam engine.

MATTHEW BAGNET

Old army friend of George Rouncewell. Although he is out of the army, he still retains much of the military manner as part of his life. He is a bluff, good-humored man, faithful to his friends.

MRS. BAGNET

Bluff, hearty, military wife of Matthew Bagnet upon whom he relies to make the decisions in their lives.

REVEREND MR. CHADBAND

A fraudulent, smooth-talking preacher (self-appointed), whose wordy and nonsensical sermons resemble those of many ineffective clergymen.

MRS. CHADBAND

Mrs. Rachael, housekeeper for Miss Barbary, Esther's aunt when Esther was a child. Much like her husband, a self-seeking and treacherous woman.

MR. BUCKET

Inspector of Police. A relentless and clever policeman who never allows his feelings to interfere with his work as a representative of an impersonal and dehumanized police system. In spite of the caricature, he emerges as a rather likable and humorous figure.

PHIL SQUOD

Crippled, but powerful assistant to George Rouncewell. A sentimental and idealized portrait of a simple but good man.

GRANDFATHER SMALLWEED

A crippled, greedy, moneylender typical of Dickens' villains (much like Uriah Heep in David Copperfield). His character is established by his bullying of his own family and his attempt to blackmail Sir Leicester Dedlock.

MR. VHOLES

Richard Carstone's attorney. Another of Dickens unfavorable legal portraits. Although he pretends to represent Richard's interests, it is obvious to everyone but Richard that his only real interest is in his own profit.

KENGE AND CARBOY

Lawyers to Mr. Jarndyce. We never meet Carboy, but "conversation" Kenge is representative of a large class of honest, well-meaning lawyers, who simply accept the confusion and outdated practices of Chancery as part of their profession without protest and without apparent understanding of its injustice.

MR. GUPPY

Articled clerk to Kenge and Carboy, Mr. Jarndyce's lawyers. A humorous, self-seeking, but confused young man who has already larded his speech with so much legal jargon that he is almost unintelligible.

KROOK

Illiterate owner of bottle, rag, and junk shop. Called the "Lord Chancellor" by his neighbors and his shop the "Court of Chancery," he is a satirical reflection of the real Chancery where legal "junk" forever accumulates and nothing is ever brought to a conclusion. His cat, Lady Jane, who forever threatens Miss

Flite's birds (Faith, Hope, etc.), serves to intensify Dickens' **satire** on Chancery.

MISS FLITE

A small, mad old woman whose long involvement in Chancery has destroyed every other part of her life. Like the birds she keeps caged (Faith, Hope, Charity), she is never to escape its toils.

MR. GRIDLEY

"The man from Shropshire" another of the victims of Chancery, who unlike most victims, is determined to resist violently the injustice of that antiquated and inhuman system.

MRS. JELLYBY

Mother of Caddy, a sharply satiric portrait of that class of Victorian philanthropists who sought to aid the poor of Africa (or any other faraway place) while ignoring the poverty around them. A good example of Mrs. Jellyby's neglect, of course, could be seen in her own family.

MR. JELLYBY

Mrs. Jellyby's neglected and suffering husband who always seems about to say something but never does. A brief but humorously touching portrait.

CADDY JELLYBY

Eldest daughter of Mrs. Jellyby, befriended by Esther, later wife of Prince Turveydrop. She is a generous, warm hearted girl who, unlike her mother, needed some visible object for her love and affection.

PRINCE TURVEYDROP

Caddy's ineffectual, but hard-working husband, son of Mr. Turveydrop, whom he had supported for years by continuing the dancing academy begun by his mother.

MR. TURVEYDROP

Prince Turveydrop's father, Caddy's father-in-law. An idle and "fashionable" old man who is supported by the efforts of his son, and later by Caddy. Actually, a sharply satiric portrait of the Prince Regent, later George IV (1820–30), leader of the dissolute Regency society.

MRS. WOODCOURT

Allan Woodcourt's mother. A humorously interesting old woman whose ambition for her son reveals the seeking after respectability and position of much of Victorian society.

ALLAN WOODCOURT

Young doctor who befriends Mr. Jarndyce, Esther, Ada, and Richard. A kind of young Mr. Jarndyce, he is a good, endlessly patient young man whose involvement in the plot seems always the product of a chance meeting.

NEMO

Latin for "no one." The assumed name of Captain Hawdon, once engaged to Lady Dedlock, father of Esther Summerson.

VOLUMNIA DEDLOCK

Poor relation of Sir Leicester Dedlock. She is a representative of that shadowy class who forever inhabit the margins of nobility, retaining the pretensions to nobility although they lack the means.

BLEAK HOUSE

CRITICAL COMMENTARY

From the beginning, Dickens' work has commanded the attention of critics who have, for the most part, been reduced to attempting to explain the reasons for his enormous popularity in spite of numerous obvious flaws in the method of his work. Among the best of the early critics was Hypolite Taine, a famous French critic of English literature and a contemporary of Dickens. He was among the first to note what later critics have come to recognize as flaws in Dickens' style and to attempt to ascertain the reasons for the peculiar power of that style. "Consider" he wrote, "the imaginative power of Dickens, and you will perceive therein the cause of his faults and his merits, his power and his excess."

Among the many faults, which Taine discovered as inherent in Dickens' style, was his "excessive imagination." This is, of course, now something of a truism, a necessary point of departure for any serious criticism of Dickens' method, since it is obvious that Dickens' characters and scenes are often "larger than life." Even "objects with Dickens take their hue from the thoughts of his characters." When Guppy informs Lady Dedlock that he has incontestable proof that Esther Summerson is really Esther Hawdon, a shrill wind howls around Chesney Wold, "the sharp rain beats, the windows rattle, mists hide the avenues, veil the points of view and move in funeral-wise across the rising grounds." Another interesting example may be seen in Dickens' description of the weather as a good omen at Mr. Boythorn's place in the country. Here the weather is always delightful, while the adjacent property at Chesney Wold is usually drenched with rain. Thus, the persons and places which Dickens considers well ordered and natural, are usually modified by adjectives connoting brightness, freshness, and vigor. Those of which he disapproves are characterized by dampness, dullness, and decay. Although Taine held these heightenings of character and place as stylistic flaws, he also argued that they were just as often the source of Dickens' power as a writer, because they helped Dickens to satirize oppressive society, and to distinguish more sharply between false happiness and false virtue.

Taine's criticism was expanded by G. K. Chesterton who argued that Dickens was not a novelist at all, but rather a pure satirist, and that the "essence of that **satire** is that it perceives some absurdity in the logic of some position," and then isolates the absurdity so all can see it. That there is some truth to this argument is, of course, obvious when we consider Dicken's exaggerated treatment of the Noodles and Doodles of English parliamentary politics in Bleak House, and his sharply satiric portraits of Mr. Turveydrop, Mr. Chadband, and Mrs. Jellyby, among others. However, more modern critics have begun to consider Dicken's work in its entirety. Instead of isolating a single volume or element such as **satire**, they have attempted to criticize Dickens' work as a whole, and to demonstrate that his work, beginning with the *Pickwick Papers*, and ending with *The Mystery of Edwin Drood*, reveals his continuous growth as literary artist and as a social critic.

Thus the major difficulty in criticism of Dickens' work appears dependent upon whether or not the critic views the work as static and essentially unchanging from one period of his life to another or whether the critic believes that the work underwent significant changes. In addition, each critic has a tendency to view Dickens through the lens of his own prejudices that either magnify his faults or virtues, or distort them in accordance with the critic's own tendencies. For example: Andre Maurois sees Dickens as a reflection of the optimistic philosophy of the English race. (There is something in this view in Taine as well.) He argues that Dickens was always looking at the bright side of life because he felt with a little kindness man could arrive at an "everlasting Christmas." This view seems essentially the same as that of Stephan Zweig, who argued that Dickens "did not write as a free artist but ... as an Anglican citizen" who did not represent an unfettered reality, but submitted for reward to the "bourgeois moral code." "This," said Zweig, "brands the whole of his work as squint-eyed hypocrisy."

These views while representative of a minority of Dickens' critics, were echoed at least in part by George Orwell. Although Orwell approved of Dickens' generally sympathetic attitude toward the poor, he found Dickens' social criticism too general and lacking in constructive suggestion. "His whole message is ... if men would behave decently the world would be decent." However, while Orwell allowed that Dickens was a social critic, he denied that he was an effective one. Thus, these criticisms, like those of T. A. Jackson (who attempted to prove that Dickens was a Marxist), appear the result of critical viewpoints that are too limited, and that fail to adequately explain the reason for Dickens' continuing popularity with all classes of readers. More sympathetic critics like Oliver Elton, Elizabeth Bowen, and George Gissing have generally agreed that Dickens was much more of a realist that he is often given credit for being, and that his characters, like Harold Skimpole; Jo, the crossing sweeper; and the brickmakers' wives, Jenny and Liz; are not totally the exaggerated caricatures they seem, revealing instead Dickens' knowledge of the devices by which the underdog lives. There can be no doubt of course, that there is much truth in these arguments, for any valid criticism of Dickens' work must be based upon a thorough knowledge of his life and of the age about which he wrote.

It appears to be the general consensus of modern critics that Dickens' work must be viewed as a whole if it is to be adequately evaluated, and critics like Edgar Johnson, Humphrey House, Monroe Engel, and A. J. O. Cockshut have added new dimensions to a clearer understanding of Dickens' life and work. As a result, Dickens has begun to emerge as more than a literary artist who was a fantastically successful novelist who totally created characters and scenes from the depths of his imagination, and was more than just a satirist. Instead, Dickens has begun to emerge as a human being, much a part of the age in which he lived and about which he wrote. He begins then to appear as a careful and conscious literary artist whose work displays evidence of serious involvement in the problems of his age, an artist whose understanding and skill grew as he matured, and finally, as an artist whose work revealed his love of humanity.

It is, then, perhaps these last concepts which have begun to explain the reasons for Dickens' success. While these critics certainly reveal an awareness of the deficiencies of Dickens' style, his use of caricature, his addiction to melodrama, the artificialities and **conventions** of plot, and his inability to portray accurately certain types of characters, they also reveal an awareness that Dickens was great enough to transcend the limitations of these deficiencies.

BLEAK HOUSE

. . . .

Question: What are some of the injustices which Dickens attacks in the course of the novel?

Answer: The first target of Dickens' **satire** is the Court of Chancery, an outmoded, unjust, and ineffectual institution whose involved procedures are like the mud and fog of the ancient London streets which surround it. It is a place filled with suitors whose cases will never be brought to proper conclusions because the Lord Chancellor and the lawyers, who are the formal representatives of England's legal system, are more interested in proper procedures than they are with human justice. First represented appropriately by Mr. Tangle, whose name describes his legal effort, and later in greater depth by Mr. Tulkinghorn, Mr. Vholes, "Conversation" Kenge, the lawyers in the novel serve only to intensify the reader's first gloomy impression of Chancery, and the hopelessness of the suitors whose cases are to be tried in it. Finally, the English legal system is satirized in the person of Inspector Bucket, who never allows human feelings to interfere with the proper performance of his duty.

The second target of Dickens is political incompetence and the fashionable society of England's ruling classes. The Doodles and Foodles of the English Parliament are, along with Sir Leicester and Lady Dedlock, (the leaders of that fashionable society who support the Doodles and Foodles), treated in numerous sharply satiric passages as a class of humans who cling to outmoded political theories and to the positions of prominence which they hold through inheritance-believing themselves superior to that great class of common men who have secured position and power through their own efforts.

A third major target of Dickens' **satire** is false charity, represented by Mrs. Jellyby, whose philanthropy only works at long range, and Mrs. Pardiggle and Mr. Quale, who believe that the way to help the poor is to read them religious pamphlets and to scold them because they are ragged and dirty.

A fourth target of Dickens' **satire** is, of course, religious hypocrisy of the kind represented by the oily Reverend Chadband, whose nonsensical sermons are a **parody** of those of a good many foolish clergymen.

Question: What are some of the techniques by which Dickens creates characters?

Answer: Dickens creates his characters in many ways. First, the key to a character's personality may be noted in the way he is described. For example: Mr. Tulkinghorn's black clothes reveal something of his personality; Mrs. Jellyby's ill-fitting clothes help us to realize her inefficient nature; and Mr. Turveydrop's "fashionable" dress reveal his interests. Second, characters may often be understood by peculiar mannerisms of their speech. Guppy speaks in an almost unintelligible legal jargon which adds to the novel's humor at the same time that it reveals his ambition; Mr. Tulkinghorn, of course, rarely speaks, which is a further clue to his ominous nature; the direct and honest speech of Mr. Boythorn and George Rouncewell reveals them as good men. A third technique of creating character is developed by allowing the places that they inhabit to reveal something of their personalities. Mr. Tulkinghorn inhabits a gloomy, ill-lighted room whose walls are covered with locked cupboards containing the secrets of his clients, in much the same manner that he keeps them locked in his mind; Chesney Wold is like its master Sir Leicester Dedlock, a moldering monument to past glories; the litter and confusion of Mr. Krook's junk shop reveal its owner's madness.

In addition to these, Dickens employs more usual means of creating characters. Often Dickens, speaking in his own person as narrator, tells us what characters are like; or, he tells us of the actions which they undertake; and by the manner in which he tells us, we approve or disapprove. For example, when we discover that Harold Skimpole has taken money from Mr. Bucket to reveal Jo's hiding place, the judgment we make of his character is not a kind one. And when Richard fails at one profession after another, we (along with Mr. Jarndyce, Esther, and Ada) feel saddened because of his weakness. Finally, characters are revealed to us when we are allowed to know their thoughts. We know, for example, that Esther and Mr. Jarndyce are good not only because of what they do, but because of the thoughts which they have.

Question: How does Dickens employ symbols to develop and intensify the **theme** of the novel?

Answer: Among the primary symbolic devices by which Dickens intensifies the novel's **theme** of the injustice of the law's delay, is the symbolic alliance of Chancery and death. All of the characters of the novel who are involved with the court of Chancery die. Richard Carstone, Mr. Gridley, Lady Dedlock, Tom Jarndyce, all die as a direct result of their involvement with that awful institution. Even Miss Flite is not exactly an exception since she is mad as the novel opens and thus participates in a kind of living death. Not only do the suitors before the Court die, but the practitioners as well; both Mr. Nemo and Mr. Tulkinghorn die; and Mr. Vholes, with his black funeral gloves, his buttoning up, and his lifeless manner reveals a kind of spiritual death.

Among the other numerous symbolic devices are: the moldering Chesney Wold a symbol of a dying way of life; the wastepaper which fills the room at Mrs. Jellyby's, symbolic of the ineffectiveness of the kind of charity which she represents; the wastepaper at Mr. Krook's shop, where the vast quantities of ancient legal documents further reinforce Dickens' criticism of the wastefulness of that institution; the squalor of Tom-All-Alone's street, which like the humans in the novel is also in Chancery; Miss Flite's birds, Faith, Hope, and Charity, are like these virtues in the Court of Chancery, hopelessly caged.

Question: How good are Dickens portraits of the upper classes?

Answer: Rarely are the characters of members of the upper classes fully realized. The Dedlocks and those who visit them at Chesney Wold and in London, are only given the briefest kind of sketches. Although it is true that, at the close of the novel, Sir Leicester Dedlock assumes some human feelings, the portrait of him which appears throughout the major portion of the book is a long-distance view. Never is the reader allowed to look into his mind, and understand the manner in which he thinks. Even the conversations that we are privileged to overhear are those with the rather simple Volumnia, or with the Doodles and Foodles, so that we never see him in a variety of situations as we do the other major characters of the novel. The same difficulty, of course, basically exists with the portrayal of Lady Dedlock. The only conclusion which is possible is that obviously Dickens was not as effective at creating characters of the upper classes since he obviously did not know them very well.

Question: What elements of melodrama are obvious in the plot of *Bleak House*?

Answer: Although the plot of *Bleak House* is well integrated with its **theme**, it is obvious that parts of it are managed at Dickens' convenience. For example: Allan Woodcourt serves always to arrive just in the nick of time, to treat poor Jo, or to help Miss Flite; and even when he arrives unexpectedly in London after a long voyage, he "accidentally" runs into Esther, who at that moment happens to be in Deal visiting Richard.

Devices like the long lost son (George Rouncewell), who returns, as if from the dead, parental objection (a variation of course when Mr. Jarndyce comes temporarily between Esther and Allan Woodcourt), and **foreshadowing** (the footsteps on the Ghost's Walk at Chesney Wold) are all devices more common to theatrical production than to the novel, yet they add much to its movement.

Question: How well does Dickens portray middle- and lower-class characters?

Answer: The portraits of middle-class characters, of professional men, and of characters like Mr. And Mrs. Snagsby (who represent a class of small tradesmen), and Jo, the crossing sweep, are more detailed and accurate than those of the upper classes. In these we are not only able to see the characters as they appear, but are able to understand how they feel, to understand and appreciate their hopes, their desires, their fears. In the detailed portraits of Mr. Jarndyce and Esther, the middle class appears as an essentially good-natured, honest class, willing to work in order to achieve the objects and the happiness which they desire. In the professional men, especially the lawyers, we become aware of a group on the edges of gentility, who strive, often honestly and earnestly (even if often mistakenly), to achieve position and honor. In the portraits of the lower classes (especially in Jo and the brickmakers and their families), we become aware of the hopelessness which makes up a large portion of their lives. Unable to get help or to help themselves, they live on the margins of bare existence, without hope of betterment, angrily resisting the attempts of inefficient do-gooders (like Mrs. Pardiggle) who only add to their misery.

It is thus, in these categories of society that Dickens appears at his best, for it was into one of these classes that he was born and lived most of his life. As a result, he understood such people so well that instead of merely creating these characters, he lived them.

Question: How is the plot as it involves Bleak House logically joined to those plot elements relating to Chesney Wold?

Answer: In the beginning of the book, Chesney Wold and Bleak House are contrasted as totally different and separate worlds. However, as the plot develops numerous connections between them are revealed which draw them closer together. First, the relationship between Esther and Lady Dedlock establishes a link which is almost immediately strengthened by Lady Dedlock's involvement in the same Chancery suit as Ada and Richard. Later, they are drawn most tightly together through Mr. Jarndyce's friendship with Mr. Boythorn, who lives next door to Chesney Wold in Lincolnshire. (Even this relationship is strengthened when, later in the novel we are informed that Mr. Boythorn had once been engaged to Lady Dedlock's sister, Miss Barbary.)

Other connections are established through common relationships with other characters, for example, through George Rouncewell who is revealed as the long-lost son of Mrs. Rouncewell, the housekeeper of Chesney Wold, and later, Mr. Guppy who is both suitor to Esther and anxious to help Lady Dedlock. Finally, the two plot strands are drawn together through common connection in the persons of Inspector Bucket and Jo, each of whom is involved with the Dedlocks as well as with the inhabitants of Bleak House.

Question: How are those elements relating to Tom-All-Alone's related to other plot elements?

Answer: Actually *Bleak House* is a novel which is written on two connected levels. The world which is inhabited by the fashionable, and the world of Tom-All-Alone's have their common relationship in the Chancery (for we are told that this desirable property is in Chancery) which is itself the product of that fashionable world's indifference. The Court of Chancery is, of course, only one aspect of the fashionable world's parliamentary failure, for it is the members of the fashionable world who legislate, who control the mechanism of government; and who are blind to the needs of everyone but themselves. Neither Sir Leicester Dedlock, nor Volumnia, nor any of the fashionable world ever talk about anything but those measures which will enable them to preserve their inherited privilege.

Indeed, a reflection of the fashionable world is mirrored in the attitudes of diverse characters like Mrs. Jellyby and Mrs. Pardiggle, each of whom in her own way somehow aspires to that world. It is revealed that the only real concern that either of them has is directed, not so much toward alleviating the ills of the poor, but to forming a kind of mutual admiration society where each can boast to the other of her accomplishments, (which are, of course, much more imagined than real). Another reflection of the attitudes of the fashionable world may be seen in Harold Skimpole, who, like so many, willingly adopts the belief and modes of the society that he admires, although he lacks its means.

Both worlds are, of course, for Dickens very real, and in *Bleak House* the connection between them is established in diverse ways. Although he never offers any positive solution to the grinding poverty of Tom-All-Alone's, he clearly implies that the election of the Ironmaster to Parliament is a step in the right direction. Then, too, he seems to say if there is to be charity, let it be like the charity of Esther and John Jarndyce, freely given without fanfare and without expectation of credit.

Question: Who are some of the humorous characters in *Bleak House* and what about them accounts for their humor?

Answer: Unlike most of Dickens' earlier novels, *Bleak House* does not contain a great deal of Dickens characteristic humor. However, the tension of the story as it unfolds is relieved in the humorous speech of Guppy, who cannot help but talk like the lawyer he hopes to be, even when such speech is inappropriate. There is also a certain amount of humor attached to the Snagsby household, where poor henpecked Mr. Snagsby is suspected of unfaithfulness by his dragon of a wife. Strangely, too, we are made to laugh at the convulsions of the unfortunate Guster, who has a habit of disrupting the household by throwing a fit whenever the overbearing Mrs. Snagsby speaks too sharply to her. Finally, Mr. Boythorn's angry and explosive explanation of his feud with Sir Leicester Dedlock, and the kindly Mr. Jarndyce's means of escaping unpleasantness, have a way of provoking the reader to a smile when the seriousness of the plot has become too intense.

Any research paper should, of course, be based on reliable texts. Among the standard editions of Dickens works are: *The Works of Charles Dickens*, 36 vols., London: Chapman, 1910–11; *The Nonesuch Dickens*, 23 vols., ed. by A. Waugh, et al., London: Nonesuch Press, 1937–38; and the Tavistock Edition, *The Works of Charles Dickens*, 36 vols., New York: Scribner, 1911. An inexpensive edition of *Bleak House* with a good introduction can be bought from Houghton Mifflin Co., Cambridge Mass. (Riverside Edition B-23).

There are innumerable biographical and critical books and articles on Dickens and his work. The following is partially annotated, alphabetically arranged list of the most important of them, arranged according to their classifications.

BIOGRAPHY, CRITICISM, AND BACKGROUND

Allen, Walter. *The English Novel*, New York: Dutton, 1954, pp. 179–198.

Baker, Ernest A. *History of the English Novel*. 10 vols. London: Witherby, 1924–39.

Cecil, Lord David. *Early Victorian Novelists*. New York: Bobbs-Merrill, 1935.

Chancellor, E. B. *The London of Charles Dickens*. New York: 1924.

Chesterton, G. K. *Criticism and Appreciation of the Works of Charles Dickens*. London: Dent, 1933.

Chesterton, G. K. *The Victorian Age In Literature*. New York: Holt, 1913.

Christie, O. F. *Dickens And His Age*. London: Heath, Cranton, 1939.

Cockshut, A. O. J. *The Imagination of Charles Dickens*. New York: New York University Press, 1962. (an excellent discussion of Dickens' symbols.)

Collins, Phillip. *Dickens And Crime*. London: Macmillan, 1962.

Crompton, Lewis. **Satire** *And Symbolism In Bleak House*. Criticism III, 1961, pp. 206–18.

Cruikshank, R. J. *Charles Dickens And Early Victorian England*. London: Pitman, 1949. (Illustrated.)

Dexter, Walter. *The England of Dickens*. Phila.: Lippincott, 1925.

Dickens, Mamie. *My Father as I Recall Him*. New York: Harpers, 1900.

Dickensian, The. *A periodical devoted entirely to Dickens*, published at monthly or quarterly intervals since 1905.

(The notes to *Bleak House* appear in Vol. XL.)

Engel, Monroe. *The Maturity of Dickens*. Cambridge, Mass.: Harvard Univ. Press, 1959. (Discusses the later work of Dickens.)

Fawcett, F. D. *Dickens the Dramatist*. London: W. H. Allen, 1952. (By S. Stokes, pseud.)

Fielding, K. J. *Charles Dickens: A Critical Introduction*. New York: Oxford, 1958. (Informative.)

Forster, John. *The Life of Charles Dickens*. Ed. B. W. Matz and annotated by J. W. T. Ley. London: Palmer, 1928. (The Ley edition is the standard biography).

Gissing, George R. *Critical Studies of the Works of Charles Dickens*. New York: Greenberg, 1924. (Among the best of the critical commentaries.)

Hayward, A. L. *The Days of Dickens*. New York: Dutton, 1926.

Holdsworth, Sir William. *Charles Dickens as Legal Historian*. New Haven: Yale, 1929.

House, Humphrey. *The Dickens World*. New York: Oxford, 1941.

Johnson, Edgar. *Charles Dickens: His Tragedy and Triumph*. 2 vols. New York: Simon & Schuster, 1952. (Excellent, adds material not in Forster.)

Kitton, F. G. *The Dickens Country*. London: A and C. Black, 1930.

Leacock, Stephen B. *Charles Dickens: His Life and Work*. New York: Doubleday, 1934. (Short, readable.)

Ley, J. W. T. *The Dickens Circle*. London: Chapman, 1919.

Miller, J. Hillis. *Charles Dickens; The World of His Novels*. Cambridge, Mass.: Harvard Univ. Press, 1958.

Orwell, George. *Dickens, Dali & Others: Studies in Popular Culture*. New York: Reynal & Hitchcock, 1946. (Good modern appreciation of the place of Dickens as a novelist.)

Pearson, Hesheth. *Dickens: His Character, Comedy, and Career*. New York: Harper, 1949.

Pierce, G. A., Wheeler, W. A. *Dickens Dictionary*. New York: Houghton-Mifflin, 1878.

Pope-Hennessy, Una B. *Charles Dickens*, 1812–1870. London: Chatto, 1934. (Informative, chatty.)

Quiller-Couch, Sir Arthur. *Charles Dickens and other Victorians*. London: Cambridge, 1935.

Van Amerongen, J. B. *The Actor in Dickens*. New York: Appleton Century, 1927.

Wagenknecht, Edward. *The Cavalcade of the English Novel*. New York: Holt, Rinehart & Winston, 1954, pp. 213–233. (Contains good bibliography.)

Wilson, Edmund. "The Two Scrooges," *The Wound and the Bow*. New York: Oxford, 1947.

Woolcott, Alexander. *Mr. Dickens Goes to the Play*. New York: Putnam, 1922.

BIBLIOGRAPHY, AND GENERAL VICTORIAN BACKGROUND

Annual Bibliography, (1922–)

PMLA. Since 1956 contains articles by English and American scholars.

Darton, J. Harvey. *Cambridge Bibliography of English Literature.* III, pp. 435–55.

Trevelyan, George M. *British History in the Nineteenth Century and After* (1782–1919). London: Longmans Green, 1922.

Illustrated English Social History. (Vol. IV, *The Nineteenth Century*), London: Longmans Green, 1952.

"Victorian Bibliography," annually in *Modern Philology*, 1933–57, and *Victorian Studies*, 1958–.

Young, G. M. (ed.). *Early Victorian England* 1830–1865. 2 vols., London: Oxford, 1934.